What Women Want

versus

The gender, transgender and cultural wars of the West

Janice Atkinson

What Women Want

versus

The gender, transgender and cultural wars of the West

Aspekt Publishers

Gender War

© Janice Atkinson
© 2019 Uitgeverij ASPEKT / Aspekt Publishers
Amersfoortsestraat 27, 3769 AD Soesterberg, The Netherlands
info@uitgeverijaspekt.nl – http://www.uitgeverijaspekt.nl

Cover: Snegina Uzunova, Mark Heuveling
Inside: Aspekt graphics

ISBN: 9789463385930
NUR: 130

All rights reserved. No reproduction copy or transmission of this publication may be made without written permission.

Contents

Preface		7
1.	The Gender Agenda I wrote this book to take on the 'gender agenda industry'	9
2.	Government and institutions	17
3.	How do you self-identify?	85
4.	The weird world of corporates and our beloved institutions have sadly fallen	93
5.	Transgender and children	111
6.	Science and de-transitioning	137
7.	Trans facts and figures from around the world	163
8.	In the mad, bad world of gender division and diversity	171
9.	Feminazism and fighting back	179
10.	My friend the Trans Woman	209
11.	My friend, Trannie	221
12.	Introduction to John, gay and happy, not transgender	229
13.	Dr Sid Lukkassen's views	237
14.	What women want and conclusion	251

Preface

A year ago, when I started this book it was going to be mainly about feminazi politics and the gender wars. Yet as I researched a larger problem loomed – transgenderism in children and the well-funded transgender industry. I explore this horrific phenomenon, where did it come from, why is it an epidemic, why are we accepting it and how do we fight back?

I explore the politics, our family structures, how it's infecting our children, our workplaces, social media, our institutions, the science behind it, the fight back, the facts and figures on transgender and chapters dedicated to people who have had the full transgender operation, a transvestite and someone who, as a teenager, was encouraged to 'trans' only to discover he was gay - only gay – how many more young people are there like him?

The trans debate has only just started in the UK because politicians were too frightened of the backlash if they spoke out against the powerful trans lobby.

The left driven media of the BBC, Guardian and Independent newspapers have been championing the acceptability of transgender and running stories that broke no criticism, only encouraging the activists.

The right-leaning media are now coming out and timidly asking the questions that should have been asked a few years ago.

Our plucky Daily Mail has been exposing the weird world of the families that encourage and indulge their children in the trans world. The Sunday Times has been running stories about the phenomenon, exposing how those who question the science and acceptability of the trans bullies have been hounded out of jobs and have had their reputations trashed.

One only has to look at the comments section of our newspapers to see what the nation really thinks.

I do believe there are people who have true body dysphoria and I cover that in this book, but I do not accept the current tsunami of people who believe they are transgender are genuine. They have other issues which I will explore.

Chapter 1

The Gender Agenda
I wrote this book to take on the 'gender agenda industry'

Find a cause – build a lobby of activists – give them TV airtime – extract cash from stupid politicians – biology and history is re-written and bullying and confusion reigns supreme

Do you feel like me, that you're living in a parallel universe of what the politically and manically correct thinks and legislates for versus the everyday lives that ordinary people lead?

Did you ever think that the word 'binary' was a mathematical term? Yet now it is used in our culture wars, deployed as a weapon against those of us who question the many varieties of sexual identities we can adopt at will, like last year's fashion trends.

Like other causes that come with a political hashtag, or indeed large amounts of funding from vested interests or the hard-pressed taxpayer, where cash is handed out like confetti at a Greek wedding, industries and campaigns grow and fester, condemning the vast majority of people who do not conform to the cultural Marxist group think world as bigots.

Whether it's the climate change industry, human rights industry, immigration industry, racism industry, legalisation of drugs industry, the same people are involved. There are many activists for each cause or they take up multiple causes, are all well-funded (many by us, the hard pressed taxpayers by out of touch governments and supra national bodies), aggressive and often, nasty bullies.

Politicians, without our approval, are turning confused young people into victims of the new Frankensteins, the gender re-assignment industry.

First, they identify a cause, usually started by a celebrity luvvie or the liberal Left. Instead of keeping us safe against terrorism, securing our borders against illegal migration, the drugs menace killing our children, organised crime, expanding employment through business friendly tax policies, ensuring our health services are fit for purpose and our children receive an unbiased and safe education, they take up causes that the ordinary voter has no concern with, has never thought about and will never concern them, but our taxes go towards funding extreme, marginal issues, that should be better dealt with by psychiatrists.

The culprits sit in chambers across the Western world and groupthink us into submission, aided by laws passed by them. The United Nations, the European Union, the Left, the Mainstream Media, Western governments, even the Anglican church, have all combined to drive an agenda that is dangerous and wrong.

The debate has moved on from nature and nurture; we're all encouraged to be gender fluid now. This creates victims. The majority of young people who seek gender reassignment have psychosocial issues and, aided by the industry that encourages them to seek sexual change, to undergo an operation will that transform their lives. Even when the Frankenstein gender industry pump them full of hormones, chop off their sexual parts and breasts, they will continue to have psychological issues. This barbarism will not resolve their psychological problems. Is it any wonder that there is an epidemic of sexually confused souls?

Let me state, at the outset, I am not opposed to gay people and I will continue to use that term throughout the book. Homosexuals and lesbians are men and women, whether you're a gay man, you're still a man, if you're a lesbian, you're still a woman. Even if you chop off your penis and pump yourself full of female hormones, you are still a man. Your gender is still your gender, it's imprinted into your DNA, that which you were born with. I believe that the current fad for trans, particularly in our children, is empowering the child, not the adults in charge.

I do believe that there are people with sexual dysphoria. There is no credible scientific research that shows children really are trans. Just because behaviour doesn't conform to rigid sexual norms it does not equate to trans either. We are jumping to conclusions based on adult diagnoses with an agenda.

It's time for us to fight back. To take on the politicians and industry which is manufacturing and trying to make socially engineered dysfunction the norm.

What is truly frightening that it is the so-called Conservative politicians across the West who are waving the right-on, politically correct flags usually reserved for the nutters on the liberal left.

In the EU, US and across the Western world we are under attack.

Our children are being indoctrinated in schools and media by the liberal Left, from the US, to Europe to Anglo Saxon nations and across the English speaking world.

Why have we allowed this creeping elitist, sexist cancer to happen? Emasculating our male children, telling them that females deserve a better chance than them, effectively pushing our sons to the back of the queue whilst we masculinise our females.

Our men are portrayed as vile sexual predators, more recently by the anti Trump women and then the Hollywood luvvies #MeToo movement who all love a march with their knitted pussyhats, clutching their chia lattes in designer trainers, some bringing their kids, or leaving them at home with their employed and underpaid migrant nannies.

We're all outraged now.

That's if you believe a small minority of middle class women, who all have degrees from third rate universities in gender/wimmin's studies courses - the new witches covens. In this book, I will rip them apart and tell our sons that this is small minded drivel from a small band of privileged shrills, which we are fighting against.

I am at the frontline of politics trying to stop them.

In the European Parliament, the gender brigade have a seat at every committee table - from feminising fishing, climate change and migration, to name but a few - they now have quotas and budgets to enforce their ideology.

I am not alone. We are seeing a backlash across Europe, in Poland the ruling PiS party is Catholic Conservative, in Hungary, Viktor Orban is doing a sterling job and they are not alone, there are millions who think like we do in the UK and US.

Recently real conservatives have been elected in Austria and Italy and Marine Le Pen and Geert Wilders are the official opposition in their respective countries.

In the US, a powerful female lobby tried to undermine President Trump's campaign and is still trying to impeach him.

Hillary Clinton, their champion, the ultimate feminazi was defeated, despite her support from the legacy media. Those in the West who supported Mr Trump were derided. I was often screeched at by the legacy media and questioned why 'a woman' was supporting a Trump presidency, I received a battering in the media.

The feminazis champion more women in politics, but it has to be the right kind of woman, not female quotas for equality (which I oppose). Whilst the lib/left adored Hillary, they reviled France's Marine Le Pen. Why could the US have Hillary as its first female president but France could not have Madame President Le Pen? The feminazis and MSM encouraged women to vote for Hillary but not Marine. Their hypocrisy is astounding.

And while the politicians and feminazis malign our menfolk and undermine our sons, we should remind them, ladies, that women bought 125 million copies of Fifty Shades of Grey.

Queer Politics

Of course, central to the feminazi theme is the transgender and LGBTQ lobby. They are now very successfully confusing our children into believing they are transgender and that adults cannot question their agenda in any way. From toilets to schools and the workplace, the emphasis is now on the intolerance of those woman who do not wish to share a toilet with a man or still giggle at the transgender men in their wigs, high heels and painted nails. We are not allowed to pity them, we must applaud their courage, their victimhood and never, ever criticise.

The liberal left create transgender celebrities, put them on a pedestal, with or without beards, just put on a sparkly dress, complete with botox, fillers, false breasts, enhanced bottoms and surgery to create a figure to die for, as if it was real and normal. Real women do not look like this, it is fantasy dressing up and demeaning to ordinary women.

Our children are confused about their gender, because they are indoctrinated about transgender.

In the UK our strapped for cash National Health Service funds transgender operations, whilst cutting funding for in-vitro fertilisation and elderly care.

We have got our priorities very wrong in the West. No wonder the Jihadis see us as easy game.

Of course, this isn't really about trans 'rights', it's part of the remorseless revolution aimed at erasing our traditional values and demonising small 'c' conservatives. That's why it's been seized upon by the hard Left, who are now aided and abetted by a right-on Conservative government, who are so desperate to be liked that they shy away from making the real case for conservatism, seeing it as too hard because they are minnow politicians.

Instead of tackling the liberal/left takeover of our educational establishments, our civil service and the state funded broadcaster, the BBC, by having a root and branch clear out, we cower to them. I know it's the same in the US, with the Clinton News Network and their printed media. And across the EU and Trudeau's Canada.

Given the cash and resources poured into gender politics, you would think that there is a huge swell of transgender people, so what are the statistics on trans people.

You will be astounded that no official government figures exist. The Office for National Statistics, the official collector of government statistics, states that it currently does not collect data, but they do have plans for the 2021 census.

According to one charity, the Gender Identity Research and Education Society, in a UK Home Office (government/taxpayer) funded study estimate the number of trans people in the UK to be between 300,000 - 500,000, defined as '... a large reservoir of transgender people who experience some degree of gender variance' (Reed et al 2009). When you consider that trans make up less than 1% of the population, there is an inordinate amount of money, laws and time taken up with this marginal subject.

I will explore how we got to this parlous state, cite the damage being done, expose those who are pushing these agendas, paint a picture of this very damaging agenda in real life stories which is now the reality of everyday life and tell politicians what women really want and it's not the same as that which is currently being forced upon us.

Chapter 2

Government and Institutions

Western governments have imposed the gender agenda on us without our consent, leading to mission creep through our institutions: the church, at all levels of education, our health service, military and the civil service

The politics and how it has impacted on ordinary people:

We have only ourselves to blame. We voted in our Western governments. Yet, we did not vote for the supra national bodies that wield enormous power and money – the European Union's institutions, the United Nations and its agencies, the World Health Organisation, the thousands of lobby companies, the liberal elite comprising the corporate globalists - Davos Man, the huge charities and NGOs who are given vast sums of taxpayers' money.

They would have you believe they are acting on our behalf. But did you vote for the faceless bureaucrats that really run our lives?

We think we vote for governments because of their manifestos. But once they get into power all manner of other issues pop up to change our societies together with the accompanying laws onto our statute books.

The EU would have you believe that you voted for me as your representative in the European Parliament. Do I have the ability to propose or repeal legislation? No, that's done by the politburo of the European Commission, the unelected body that proposes damaging and societal changing laws. And if the MEPs have the temerity to vote down a law, then it is recycled, regurgitated and spat out again until we vote the right way, their way. A subject is never dropped.

Did the EU and the UK as individual nation states vote for gender quotas, diversity, multiculturalism, uncontrolled migration and Islamic terror? No. But the current UK faux Conservative government is altering our society in ways that runs concurrent with the barmy ideas that originate in the EU.

Many of the gender, diversity and LGBTQ+ ideas originate from the extreme Left/communists, Greens and socialists that sit in the EU Parliament. Many of their dangerous ideas are often rubber stamped by the liberals and the conservative left because they want to be seen as right-on progressives. And, as they can outvote the conservative right (at this moment), they win. These laws are then passed onto the nation states' statutes with no right to amendment or rejection because of the Treaties.

In the US, if you are Californian and have a son or daughter or you are a single sexually active person, do you think that it is ok for Governor Jerry Brown to decriminalise those who knowingly infect others with HIV? But allow criminals to smoke in a park?

The only governments in the world that are now supporting traditional family life are the populists – Trump, an increasing number of Eastern EU states, Australia, Japan and some other naturally conservative nations. It is not a coincidence that the European Parliament and the EU Commission are seeking to punish the former communist countries through their EU courts.

How did we get into this parlous state?

In the UK Parliament, we have the Commons Women and Equalities Select Committee and even a government minister dedicated to gender equalities (note, not equality, but equalities, plural).

In the UK, we have a Conservative government, apparently, but only in name, not in attitude and values.

This committee recently produced a report saying that transgender people are being failed. They ignored the medical evidence that young people who are confused about their gender need psychiatrists and counsellors who could guide them through their mental and sexual conflicts. Instead, the UK government funds 'gender counsellors' who encourage our children to confirm their confused thoughts.

The woman who heads up this waste of time committee, was a government minister in charge of sexuality and is a Conservative MP, Maria Miller, someone who I encountered some years ago when we were budding candidates running for election. Back then she was unassuming and did not seem to have strong views one way or the other on anything, indeed, perfect fodder for David Cameron who was then Leader of the Opposition. She is now a dangerous subversive and I will tell you why.

Her committee wishes to dump the medical evidence of confused gender and now claims that by denying the many varieties of sexuality it 'pathologises trans identities' and runs 'contrary to the dignity and personal autonomy' of trans people. They acknowledge a UK survey that found about half of young and a third of adult transgender people said they had attempted suicide.

Instead of concluding that their mental conflict over their sexuality was the problem, they blamed 'transphobia'.

Instead of increasing the number of mental health practitioners to help these poor souls, they concluded that schools should include gender issues on the curriculum as part of 'personal, social and health' education. Inevitably, this will lead to gender fluidity and will be actively promoted as normal and a lifestyle choice. Anyone who then disagrees will be cited as bigots and, eventually, arrested and convicted of hate crime. This will lead to more cash and fodder for the human rights industry and fewer real criminals being caught and punished.

At the time of going to print, this committee has produced the Gender Recognition Bill, which seeks to amend the 2004 Act and has just finished its consultation, which was extended because of the sheer number of people who were outraged by its proposed change in law. It remains to be seen who wins – the well-funded and active trans lobbyists or the ordinary people. I know quite a number of Conservative

MPs who are very angry, let's see if they make their voices heard in public.

The consultation states:

"Trans people are able to receive legal recognition of the acquired gender … only 4,910 people have changed their gender … this is fewer than the number of trans respondents to the government's LGBT survey … who wanted legal recognition … but found the current process too bureaucratic, expensive and intrusive …".

In the consultation document the government openly states they don't know how many trans people there are in the UK, yet they are pandering to a tiny minority who find it inconvenient to go through the correct procedures for recognition.

At the moment a person can change their gender by:

1. A medical diagnosis of gender dysphoria
2. A report from a medical professional detailing any medical treatment
3. Proof of having lived for at least two years in their acquired gender through, for example, bank statements, payslips and passport
4. A statutory declaration that they intend to live in the acquired gender until death
5. If married, the consent of their spouse
6. Submission of a low fee of £140 and submission of said document to a Panel, which the applicant does not meet in person

The Ministerial Foreword by the Minister, Penny Mordaunt, states:

"We have introduced a £3m project to help tackle transphobic bullying in schools; we have put more money into the NHS Gender Identity Services ... reported hate crime is rising ... reported self-harm and suicide rates, particularly among young trans people, are extremely concerning ... to be clear – this this is an explorative consultation and we do not have all the answers".

And there we have it, a document that doesn't know what the answers are, that the small number of people who have changed their legal gender is small yet, surprise surprise, the amount of people who responded – in their tens of thousands – will have been urged on by the powerful trans lobby.

Note the money already spent in schools. This is not to stop 'bullying' this is to promote the trans agenda into our children's young minds. That £3m would have been better spent on teaching STEM subjects.

The Minister is right to be concerned about self-harm and suicide rates, nearly all of which is directly attributable to the government and the trans terrorists who encourage transgender rather than treating it as a mental illness or stopping our children being subjected to the dangerous information available.

The European Parliament Committee on Women's Rights and Gender Equality - FEMM (sic) committee

When elected as a Member of the European Parliament my main objective was to oppose every piece of legislation brought forward by the unelected EU Commission (unless it repatriated powers or returned money to the UK) and campaign for Brexit.

For a short time, I joined the FEMM (Women's Rights and Gender) committee. There were a few brave conservatives who fought their deeply damaging nonsense but we were always in the minority. From Angela Merkel's so-called conservatives to the alt-left, we were fighting a losing battle because we were always outvoted either in committee or eventually during the voting sessions.

I left this committee, for my own sanity and to concentrate on the biggest battle of all, Brexit, which we won.

However, during my time on the La La Land of the FEMM committee world it really was an alt-universe made up of economically illiterate feminazis, hell bent on an agenda so alien to the family, business, men, our sons and normal women.

Let me quote the following opening welcome remarks by the 'chair' (a socialist) on the home webpage: *"Despite many successes in empowering women, numerous issues still exist in our social, cultural, political, and economic life where women are not equally treated. Our general concerns are voiced namely over pay gap, women's economic independence, female poverty, women's underrepresentation in decision making, sexual and reproductive health rights, trafficking and violence against women and girls. We want to bring a change and mainstream gender into all EU policies. In order to do this, we need the help of civil society and all organizations who contribute to the engagement for equal rights for all."*

All sounds great doesn't it? What's not to like? I will now deconstruct.

Gender quotas

Not content with being elected by their voters, the committee members decided that gender quotas should be imposed in politics and business.

Some of the committee recently travelled to the UN and opined the lack of gender equality in the digital economy. Now, the last time I looked, girls were taught IT in schools. The digital economy, a relatively new economy, is vibrant, fast moving and doesn't see sex, sorry gender, as a barrier. Yet, one of the speakers commented on her upcoming report: "... report on economic empowerment of women in private and public sector which will focus on recommendations for improved work-life-balance conditions, mechanisms to reach equal pay for equal value work such as wage mapping, gender quotas and gender equality plans, but also pointing out the important role of collective agreements and social partners."

And there you have it, perfectly encapsulated in the phrases above: work-life-balance conditions, mechanisms to reach equal pay for equal value work such as wage mapping, gender quotas and gender equality plans, but also pointing out the important role of collective agreements and social partners.

How on earth can you encourage a vibrant, fast growing and competitive sector when all of the above have to be tick boxed?

When I call my phone provider or a bank I am generally transferred through to India where I speak to a highly educated young woman who is grateful for the transfer of business from western countries who are all arguing over the work life balance and gender quotas. Meanwhile, India is racing ahead in the digital world. Whereas the EU, despite the frustrations of the various politicians pushing the digital economy, agonise over feminazi issues. It's holding them back.

Meanwhile, the UK is racing ahead with our own digital economy, which is feared by the EU. With low corporation tax, educated girls and boys, we are attracting the big tech companies, not the EU. Yet, we could do better if teachers were not bogged down on gender issues.

The feminazis are obsessed of getting women working - whether they want to or not - I believe it is about choice, they think it is about quotas and punishment.

Their statements in 'trafficking and violence against women and girls' is laudable and something I agree with but in the context of the European Union we are talking about the migrants they have voted to let in that practice slavery and people trafficking. This practice was stamped out in Europe two hundred years ago. Yet, through their blinkered open-door immigration policies we have opened our borders to abhorrent practices from the third world.

And 'sexual and reproductive health rights' refers to conservative Catholicism which is practiced across the EU, particularly in the former Eastern bloc countries. They believe pushing abortion rights is more important than supporting families.

Try telling the newly arrived Muslim men that their women's sexual rights have nothing to do with them, or that arranged marriage, female genital mutilation and child sexual exploitation is wrong.

They laud the fact that 60% of EU graduates are women and more women are in work, but:

'The employment rate for women reached an all-time high of 64% in 2015, while 76% of men were at work. Women are four times more likely than men to engage and remain in part-time work; three quarters of household work and two thirds of parental care were performed by working women.' They actually discuss who should be doing the hoovering and dusting in Parliament.

Unpack these statistics and you will find that a number of female graduates have taken economically useless degrees such as gender studies, film studies and sociology linked courses. Yet they gloss over the fact that in the UK we have more girls reading biology, medicine and law than the boys. Is it any wonder that the former sociology lecturer, now High Commissioner for Trade, one Cecilia Malmstrom, is a product of this new political groupthink? This is the woman tasked with conducting trade deals. Is it no wonder that TTIP (US/EU trade deal) was abandoned after three decades of negotiations? Or that the EU has failed to negotiate free trade agreements with most of the world's dynamic economies?

Ms Malmstrom is a former sociology lecturer in her native Sweden, who is now in charge of trade. Yes, you read correctly, trade. I always point this out in the Parliament when speaking about trade relations with external countries.

She has failed to sign a trade agreement with any major world economy. Although she did manage to push through the deeply flawed Canadian/EU trade agreement, CETA.

If the EU is so committed to trade deals why did it not appoint someone from a business background that is up to the job, rather than a former sociology lecturer? Yes, you've guessed it, she's a gender quota. She is symptomatic of quotas and its failures.

A couple of years ago, I attended a seminar on gender quotas in politics and business.

The woman presenting the case for quotas was failed prime minister and socialist Gordon Brown's favourite pollster, a woman called Deborah Mattison.

Her polling company had conducted extensive research into men and women's (no trans consulted back then) attitudes to gender quotas.

She found time and time again that men and women (sadly), from all social classes in business and in politics rejected quotas. Unsurprisingly, only those working in the public sector were amenable to this, probably because of the brainwashing and political correctness imposed in a culture of fear. And with the upper echelons of those employed by the taxpayer to deliver services, are generally from the rotten end of our university system with useless degrees who control the group think mentality amongst its workers.

She turned to her audience – mostly female, middle class, educated and mostly conservative – and said, 'well, what do you make of that, astounding really, how do we change their minds?'. Of course, our answer didn't chime with her analysis.

And that response is symptomatic of the political elite. How do we change their minds? Since that seminar people like her from the left, the elite, the useless holders of bad degrees, those who have been elected on a so-called conservative ticket, have managed by stealth to change our laws, to inflict their poisonous doctrine on the masses because the masses have trusted our politicians to deliver. And if they can't change our minds, they do it anyway and make it a hate crime to challenge them.

That trust is now broken. Across the Western world, the people are fighting back. First Brexit – where we triumphed against the swamp filled political elite, against a Brussels machine that spends more money on campaigns than Coca-Cola, a beast that insidiously seeps into our schools, universities and law. Our government did its best and spent millions on anti-Brexit propaganda but we won.

In the US, the clever people elected Donald Trump. They were fed up with the swamp-filled Washington elite, whose commander in chief was Obama.

In the week of the US 2016 election I was in New York to campaign for Trump. I spoke to many people about the election. From the preppily dressed upper middle class young people at a Manhattan polling station, who were queuing to vote – all were voting for The Donald (myth busted that the middle classes didn't vote Trump), to the woman at the British Airways check-in desk, on spotting my enormous piece of luggage, asked if I was leaving the country because of the Trump presidency? I replied, no, I wished I was staying, I would have voted for him. She jumped down from behind the desk, embraced me, and personally escorted me to the front of the queue for security and customs. (I didn't like to tell her I was travelling business so I had privileges anyway).

With time to spare, a woman goes shopping. As I tried the creams in Duty Free, a sales woman of Chinese origin approached me. We chatted about creams and then the election. She said she had voted for Trump because she didn't believe in Obama care. Hardly surprising when the US Department of Health Services review board ruled that Medicare can pay for transgender surgeries.

My various taxi drivers, who were mainly newish Muslim migrants, told me they were all voting for Trump. Why? Because they were ambitious, Trump was a successful businessman, they were small businessmen and knew they could make it in Trump's America.

Hillary, on launching her book of her failed election, still refuses to apologise to the women she insulted who voted for Trump.

She said "[Women] will be under tremendous pressure – and I'm talking principally about white women. They will be under tremendous pressure from fathers and husbands and boyfriends and male employers not to vote for 'the girl',"

Did this arrogant, chattel of a former womanizer, ever stop to think that these women had a choice and chose to vote for Trump? Apparently not, according to Michelle Obama and a recent report on how women vote.

Not to be left out, Michelle Obama recently said women who voted for Donald Trump over Hillary Clinton went against their "authentic voice". "Any woman who voted against Hillary Clinton voted against their own voice … What does it mean for us as women that we look at those two candidates, as women, and many of us said, that guy, he's better for me, his voice is more true to me … Well, to me that just says you don't like your voice. You like the thing you're told to like."

The truth that Hillary and Michelle will not acknowledge is that the women who bore the most resemblance to Clinton – white, heterosexual and married – were less likely to vote for her. Only 54% of women did vote for her.

Their arrogance and entitlement is backed up by an 'assistant professor' at Oregon State University and author of a recent study examining women's voting patterns states:

"We know white men are more conservative, so when you're married to a white man you get a lot more pressure to vote consistent with that ideology."

"Women consistently earn less money and hold less power, which fosters women's economic dependency on men …

Thus, it is within married women's interests to support policies and politicians who protect their husbands and improve their status." How patronising.

A college-educated woman identifying as a liberal Democrat confided to the researcher as a Trump voter – that she had voted for him over Clinton because her husband's job depends on the coal industry; she saw Trump as the candidate that would protect it, and by extension her family's economic interests. In other words, her choice, based on an economic decision affecting her family. The researcher remarked, "the clearest, most heart-breaking validation of our article that I had ever heard".

The report went on to say that single women tend to vote with other women in mind.

It is truly incredible that the liberal left are paid to write this nonsense, to come up with statements masquerading as empirical fact to support their arguments. This is ludicrous, insulting and wrong.

Do they not stop to consider that people vote in their best interests – whether that is theirs, their families or their husband's jobs? Throughout the report they refer to 'straight' women. See the thread here? They weight their arguments by overemphasising women's sexuality – a tiny minority of which are lesbian or trans. And they always bring race into the argument which, when bundled together has now become 'identity politics'.

Hillary and Michelle should just accept the fact that they lost, big time, because women rejected their politics and

Trump resonated with them more. Sweet justice and revenge for the right. We don't vote with our vaginas, we vote with our minds.

EU's obsession of getting women out of the home and into work

They are obsessed with women working and will not be satisfied until they have almost 100% employment. They never consider that women have a choice. They believe that families should place their babies in nurseries from a young age, paid for by the state, and go back to work. Usually, the nurseries are staffed by young, undereducated women on minimum wage. They do not believe that women (or men) can be stay at home parents. I make the distinction because I do not believe raising a family is gender biased. If economics dictate that the father stays at home, I have no problem with this. If the parents believe that one parent should stay be a homemaker who are politicians to dictate otherwise?

If they really want to increase the numbers of women in the workplace or at least raise their salaries, then why do they insist on flooding our countries with low paid, third world, uneducated migrants?

The EU justifies their immigration policy by citing the low birth rates in our countries and our increasingly ageing population. They gloss over the fact that there is nigh on 50% youth unemployment across many EU countries. Could the low birth rate be directly linked to their gender equality policies? If insisting women go out to work then of course they would have fewer children because it would be too exhausting.

If women choose to work part-time economics will dictate that they have lower pensions and lower incomes.

The statistics are skewed. In their world they overlook the fact that there are only ten countries of the 28 EU strong bloc who pay more in contributions than they take out. Only a few years ago only four countries paid net contributions, including the UK. Many are former communist countries who are trying to catch up with their advanced Western capitalist rivals and battle against the pervasive liberal, anti-business, anti-Catholic and anti-family agenda of the EU.

Conservatives need to fight back to say that raising children should be the prerogative of parents, to promote freedom of choice for families, through the tax system to spend as they wish on childminders, nurseries or care by a family member. Or, if they wish, to use those allowances to stay at home - whichever parent decides to do so.

Unfortunately, as most of the committee are economically illiterate or have never had a proper job in business, they have no real experience of commerce and the dynamics of economics.

They also turn their guns on the boardrooms of private or publicly listed companies.

In 2015 in the UK we rejected a proposal by the European Commission that would oblige FTSE companies to make 40 per cent of their boards female.

But as I warned at the time, although we rejected it this time, no proposed legislation ever goes away. Dirty lobbying deals are done behind closed doors and it comes back, re-packaged, re-presented as something different, but the core principle is the same.

The FEMM committee is obsessed with quotas. Instead of looking at our education system and seeing if girls are being left behind or women in the workplace are not promoted fairly on merit, or put in charge of staff or P&L balance sheets, the liberal left prefer quotas as the most offensive and blunt instrument to use for their social and cultural totalitarianism.

As I often cite, a man or woman operating the check-out in Tesco or Wal-Mart is not obsessing about the gender make-up of the boardroom. Instead, they are thinking about their next vacation or what they might feed their kids that night, or how they are going to pay for the utility bills, stuffed full of green taxes.

Instead of concentrating on marginal issues and interfering with family structures, they should be concentrating on the high unemployment rates across the EU and the effects of mass uncontrolled migration.

The assault on family structures - it's all the fault of populism!

Not satisfied in undermining our businesses and women in the workplace, those lovely ladies and some right-on, misguided men, insist on taking the oppressed struggle to our wombs and our reproductive health, even funding an outfit of NGOs, 'Promoting sexual & reproductive health & rights in a time of growing populism'. http://www.eurongos.org/home.html

This well-funded weird think tank is indicative of the EU and the cancer that is spreading across the world.

They directly link President Trump's withdrawal from the Paris Climate Change Agreement (yo! Trump, I say), as having a damaging effect on third world women's reproductive rights. What right has the West over anyone's reproductive rights?

'Populism' is defined by our enemies as President Trump, Australian and Canadian conservatism and, of course, the rise in popularity of the real conservatives in the European Parliament, those of us who are Eurosceptic, against the failing euro currency, that believe in the sovereignty of the nation state and the desire to control our own borders. Some of us are economic libertarians, some are more protectionist or more liberal in our social attitudes but what unites us is our opposition to the politics of the liberal left of the EU, Obama, Soros, Trudeau, Merkel and Macron.

Populism is taking control of countries such as Poland and Hungary. Deeply conservative and Catholic countries, they are joined by Slovakia, the Czech Republic and Romania in their opposition to the breaking up and undermining of family structures. Italy has recently joined the ranks of family based Catholicism taking back control in the form of Matteo Salvini.

The FEMM committee has a particular dislike of Catholicism and its views on reproductive health, along with another of my committees, the LIBE committee which is responsible for migration, borders, human rights and security.

They fail to recognise that despite Soviet rule, Catholicism was deeply embedded in those countries. So when a Polish colleague of mine recently spoke against the implementation of gay marriage, making the decent and honest case that they needed more time and more education to change attitudes, he was shouted down as a bigot, by a liberal Swedish MEP saying that she did not want to breath the same air as this despicable creature. Who was the despicable one?

I was at a top level meeting of the leaders of the political groupings in the Parliament, representing my group at the Conference of Presidents. The agenda turned to the populists currently elected in Poland. The female German leader of the alt-left/Green group condemned the Polish government, then headed by a woman, over their stance on abortion and reproductive rights.

I told her to stay out of the directly elected Polish government's policies. In addition, that the Poles and I do not want her or anyone else telling us what we can and cannot do with our wombs.

The ruling PiS party and the Catholic Church had been working together to change current abortion laws.

The law signed off by the Polish president, Andrzej Duda, in defiance of human rights groups and European medicines agency guidelines turns emergency contraception into a prescription drug. And what's wrong with that? Drugs have side effects and girls sometimes use the morning after pill as contraception, which is damaging to health and dangerous.

In addition, women and girls aged 15 and over will now need to make an appointment with a doctor. Polish campaigners and MEPs in Brussels say the change will have the greatest impact on rape victims and those living in isolated areas of the country.

The Dutch liberal MEP, Sophie in 't Veld, said the legislation was a violation of shared European values.

"The current populist national-conservative Polish government is enforcing a sexual counter-revolution, against the health interests and wishes of Polish women and girls," she said.

"Restricting access to the morning-after pill, combined with the right of doctors to refuse treatment based on religious grounds, will have far reaching consequences."

The trouble with Ms in't Veld, is that she and her liberal friends think anyone that doesn't agree with them is wrong and change has to be imposed.

Whether you agree or disagree with contraception, abortion or Mr Trump's stance on Planned Parenthood, the point is that the liberal left is intolerant of cultures that do not fit into their idea of social norms.

Interestingly enough, the current socialist Maltese government, which has a total ban on abortion, is not condemned or even mentioned in their tirades. It's just the populists.

UK regulated thought and an Orwellian future

The new normal, an 'Extremist Commission' is to be set up by the UK government to, "support the government in stamping out extremist ideology in all its forms". But it will also be given the task of supporting the public sector and civil society in "promoting pluralistic British values and reducing tolerance of extremism".

All good, you might think. But 'supporting civil society .... and reducing intolerance'? Instead of tackling the jihadis, I can see this leading to more tentacles encircling and strangling the intolerance of the gender agenda brigade with extremism being hurled at those of us who think that children are best brought up by a mother and a father, and that men who transition to women or vice versa are not true versions of their assigned agenda. That could be considered extremist in this brave new world of 'tolerance'.

As I have said, I have no problem with civil partnerships but I do not think a place of worship such as a church should be made to sanction gay marriage. Again, is this extremist thought? Are they going to make the Mosques initiate same sex marriage?

There has to be a backlash against the middle class liberal elite, those with the loudest voices and bigger pockets, aided and abetted by the liberal media, who have a stranglehold over our culture and society.

This will be another curtailment on freedom of speech and then thought.

Homosexuality v gender reassignment

The woman who was formerly in charge of UK gender legislation is Justine Greening, another dangerous woman. She is a so-called, 'conservative' and served as both Secretary of State for Education and Minister for Women and Equalities. She is also a lesbian.

Nothing wrong in being a lesbian, nor in charge of education, but what is worrying is that to coincide with the 50th anniversary of the UK's 1967 legalisation of homosexuality act, she decreed that making gender reassignment is a matter of simple self-declaration on forms (which is currently being consulted on in the Gender Recognition Act revision) - which is an extreme Left wing ideology where they believe gender is a social construct rather than a biological fact.

She decided that people are free to change their birth certificate, regardless of medical opinion and the tackle with which they were born. Her 'thoughts' are that whether you are a biological man or a woman is irrelevant, merely a feeling, an inner belief, which transcends biology and DNA. We may soon have a law which enables you to put an X on your passport instead of M or F.

This former minister has lost her way as a conservative and what is truly worrying is that she was also in charge of our young people's education - and thus young, impressionable minds - and as we have seen both in the US and UK, there is a dangerous element to normalise those who have troubled minds and seek gender reassignment, making it the new normal. It isn't. It's just another social justice warrior battle.

Her colleague, one Maria Miller (who we have mentioned before), who chairs the UK Parliament's 'equalities committee', said "we're not doing enough for people who have no gender at all". I don't know whether she is thick, deliberately obtuse or really believes this stuff, but we are either born male or female. Fact. Self-declaration doesn't make you something else.

In the UK it is becoming a tick box exercise to change your gender depending on which way the wind is blowing. Take the Driving Vehicle Licensing Agency. If you want to change your sex online, that's fine, just tick the box and log out. But try amending the number plate on your car and you encounter a hoop jumping exercise via postal services, postal orders and form filling.

How do you impose this cultural Marxism? – de-sex them via the official census

This faux Conservative government is now proposing that the UK becomes one of the first countries in the world not to require its citizens to declare their sex on the official census forms.

Believing that it discriminates against transgender and other non-binary people it will leave the UK without an accurate figure for the number of men and women living in our country.

Ahead of the 2021 UK census, a report has been written for government by the wonderfully right-on 'persons' – probably with a first class degree in gender studies, from a rotten university, on recommendations of gender/sex to be included in the census said, "…. that the existing census question should not be mandatory, for the benefit of particularly intersex and non-binary people who cannot choose male or female as a reflection of their current sex or gender".

I can see a pattern forming. It is vital to have a breakdown of the sex of the nation – from health, to education to planning, where an accurate number of males and females is key. If you do not collect the data on sex, thus removing all mention of male and female, then the radical feminazis and trans campaigners win. They will use their own 'statistics' to make the spurious case for more funding, more attention and recognition.

The UK census, launched in 1801 is to count people. It has served us well, we should not allow a minuscule minority to re-write public policy.

The real feminists, who were campaigners for women's rights in the 1970s, are outraged. Germaine Greer said: "…biological women were "losing out everywhere, I'm sick and tired of this. We keep arguing that women have won everything they need to win. They haven't even won the right to exist."

It is faux conservativism as it goes against the very grain of what conservatism is - the tried and tested policies based on what has historically been tried and has worked and based on our culture. It's up to the Left to be progressive and reactionary, not us conservatives.

I am afraid that the British Conservative party has lost its way. Rather than bothering to explain to young people the benefits of conservatism, just like they do in the US, this lot of career, done nothing politicians, who really don't get out into the real world as often as they should, they steal the extreme Left's ideas in the hope that the young, impressionable ABC of the LBGTQI will vote conservative. They will not. The young have had their minds indoctrinated by the Left, by teachers, public sector policies, successive governments caving into liberalism and political activism, our universities have been hi-jacked and the EU has their all pervasiveness rubber stamped into our consciousness so that to argue makes us illiberal bigots. They know the real thing when they see it and it's the Left's policies that are brought forward by the politics of the ideological war that we conservatives have almost lost, that they buy into as their minds have been indoctrinated.

The trouble is, they're not conservatives so they cannot explain why conservatism is better.

In the guise of anti terror extremism our priests and vicars are censored

In tackling Islamic extremism, the UK government instructs our schools to vet the speeches and prayers of any visiting preacher, including those mild mannered vicars from the Church of England and Catholicism.

It may be that as a parent or someone who is secular you may not wish the visiting priest to oppose gay marriage or abortion or promote marriage. But, if you're like me, you think this is part of our cultural heritage and has a place for discussion and contemplation, you may want your child to be part of that discussion. The problem with the Anglican and Catholitc churches is that they too have been infected with liberal 'values'. We have a Pope preaching that uncontrolled immigration is good while the Anglican church undermines itself by taking up a liberal left agenda. No wonder the pews in the Anglican church are declining.

The government, in falling over itself to be seen as treating everyone equally, fails to acknowledge that it is a tiny minority of lunatics that are preaching hate in our Islamic schools and mosques. It isn't the subversive men with dog collars who are the preachers or hate, extremism or encourage the bombing of the rest of us infidels.

Our schools should not be forced to reveal this information to government.

I also challenge the feminazis to start protecting our women and girls and the migrant women and children against child sexual exploitation, female genital mutilation, under-age marriage, arranged marriages and sex attacks.

They are extraordinarily quiet on these issues, preferring instead to pander to the #MeToo culture and attack our men and boys for decades old 'sex' crimes.

The British government is to become a sex pest

The latest mad idea from the British National Health Service is to ask us all routinely at every face-to-face consultation about our sexual orientation.

Like our US cousins, we can be belligerent. We are mostly easy going, we mostly lead our lives according to the law, we mostly bring up our kids to know right and wrong and we are generally fair to those who have difficult lives.

But now, faced with discussing our sexual orientation on a routine visit to the doctor for a sore throat, some birth control pills, or to consult on a potentially fatal illness, the over worked health practitioner will now ask us our sexual preferences.

This is an invasion of privacy for all, embarrassing and difficult for some and time wasting by all involved. And each GP consultation is only schedule for ten minutes. Time is money and health.

I recently oversaw a visit to the European Parliament of twenty constituents ranging from 30-80 years old. Out of the ridiculously numerous questions and data required before letting them into the Parliament one question annoyed everyone – 'what is your gender?'.

The information obtained by our health service will be used for what? This is a further invasion of privacy and bean counters wasting time inputting useless data.

LGBT people do have higher rates of suicide, mental health issues and drug and alcohol abuse. There are more subtle ways of helping people than lumping the whole 65 million of Brits into bean counting and questioning their sexual preferences.

If marriage has become an outdated concept how do we reverse that? If we are to appeal to families and conservatives, then let's do it through the tax system

There is a way to fight back. Conservatives should be giving families the support they need through the tax system.

In the UK we give a paltry £200 tax relief to married couples. Most people do not even bother claiming for it. It was a sop by the so-called conservatives to rally their grassroots supporters (leaflet and door knocking fodder).

Divorce is falling, thankfully, but nearly half of all babies are born to unmarried parents. These parents are three times more likely to split up than their married equals before their child reaches 16.

Marriage is not just a piece of paper. It is the best guarantee against family breakdown, children achieve better at school and we live longer and are happier (on the whole!).

We believe in individual choice. So give us the cash in tax relief to make those choices whilst at the same time shout out in your manifestos that you support the family structure and be proud of that, instead of filling a manifesto void of ideas full of Left lunacy.

If you do not then the Left will appeal with the magic money tree promises.

Terrorism is everything to do with toxic masculinity

The feminazis have turned their guns on appeasing terrorism. The feminazis have become apologists for the jihadi attacks instead of calling them what they are: radicalized young men, bred on a diet of hate, most with mental illness, drug taking and with an ethnic background in Islam and the Middle East. Blaming testosterone, misogyny, and 'attacks on young girls and women' is wrong. Singling out females is saying we don't care that our men, brothers, fathers and male friends died in these attacks too. It's all about gender segregation, seeing women as higher victims than men.

Determined to stick to a narrative of love trumps hate, keeping calm, carrying on, demonstrating kindness and understand through the lighting of candles, offering candles and teddy bears, they try to shut down on debate on the murderers.

Moving the argument to misogyny traduces the horrific acts. It's not Muslims likely to kill you, it's men, they say. They won't discuss how Islam is the most misogynistic religion on earth, there is no discussion on women's roles in hard line Muslim states – there are laws against that.

After the terror atrocities in Paris, London, Manchester, Cologne, Miami, California et al, the feminazi commentariat were quick to criticise any discussion on the ethnicity of the perpetrators, preferring to blame their gender. They call it 'toxic masculinity' it lies in 'male entitlement and structures that promote masculine supremacy'. Yet, these wimmin are silent in their condemnation of Radical Islam.

Our politicians encourage this group think because they do not have the guts and policies to take on the fifth column that sleeps, eats and lives amongst us.

Segregation is ok, as long it's for the religion of peace

The Islamic Education and Research Academy hosted an event on University College London premises where the seating was segregated by gender. The Snowflake, alt-left wing National Union of Students, would oppose that, right? Wrong. The spokesman for King's College, London said, "gender segregation should be respected, if not tolerated, in institutions of higher education".

Their spokesperson Shaheen Sattar, said the "stench of Islamophobia" had been "masked with feminism" in politicians' criticisms of gender segregation". If they believe in their version of feminism then gender segregation in any form is incompatible with their beliefs.

However, free speech for conservatives is not. That fact that British universities support gender apartheid is ok - as long as you're Muslim. This is totally unacceptable and the feminists should be shouting loud and clear - it's not ok, this is not respecting the Suffragette movements, this is disrespecting why our fathers and grandfathers died in two world wars, for our freedoms, this goes against everything that the sensible 1970s feminists worked for and we have reaped the benefits of.

I don't have a problem with segregation by choice. Men or women having a supper club, golf club or gym membership or having a discussion where they felt that the topics of discussion would make the opposite sex uncomfortable or perhaps discussing topics that they would only feel comfortable with the same sex.

Toxic Feminism

In the US, a woman who is fast becoming a bit of an icon to the conservatives in the UK is Kellyanne Conway. She's now in the White House but I have been following her thinking for some while.

All women in public life (and in the UK, men too) have to answer the question, Are you a Feminist?

She answered a Q&A in the Washington Post, thus:

Q: You don't consider yourself a feminist?
A: I don't consider myself a feminist. I think my generation isn't a big fan of labels. My favorite label is mommy. I feel like the feminist movement has been hijacked by the pro-abortion movement or the anti-male sentiments that you read in some of their propaganda and writings. I'm not anti-male. One does not need to be pro-female and call yourself a feminist, when with it comes that whole anti-male culture where we want young boys to sit down and shut up in the classroom. And we have all of these commercials that show what a feckless boob the man in the house is. That's not the way I see the men in my life, most especially my 12-year-old son. I consider myself a postfeminist. I consider myself one of those women who is a product of her choices, not a victim of her circumstances.

http://thefederalist.com/2017/01/31/mother-son-kellyanne-conway-gets-feminism-become-toxic/

"I consider myself one of those women who is a product of her choices, not a victim of her circumstances".

On US campuses the debate is no different to ours in the UK.

Women on college campuses spouting toxic feminism should consider whether modern feminism is helping advance their position or whether they should pursue their hopes and dreams on their own terms, as described by Kellyanne?

US campuses encourage women's involvement in a Day Without a Woman and boycotting Twitter in protest against the Harvey Weinstein's of this world. Yet, did anyone notice they were boycotting? Did anyone care? No, only the narrow self-declared and self-selected noticed. They couldn't event speak to each other as they were part of a boycott.

As in the UK, students are encouraged to rack up student debt college fees. How on earth do gender studies advance a career or even make you employable in the normal workforce, apart from some NGO funded, waste of space charity, preaching the usual nonsense against men?

Women on US colleges are told how the world of work is stacked against them; how they are victims of the patriarchy before they've even earned a cent; who are told you are paid less than men (factually incorrect) and that they should be angry.

It has always struck me how the liberal left are always angry.

The US is allowing its campuses to be places where free speech and interpretation is banned.

Why do they allow people like Joe Biden, Condoleezza Rice and even Christine Lagarde – the left leaning, tricky head of the International Monetary Fund – to be banned from campus?

OK, I can understand finding Lagarde's views unpalatable but go and debate her, don't hide.

At Yale, a recent survey of students showed that 42% of students (and 71% of conservatives) say they feel uncomfortable and targeted by giving their opinions on race, religion, gender and politics.

Instead, the minority of free speech haters are winning. These activists are demanding that more courses and time should be given to mandatory ethnic studies courses, preferential hiring of coloured or LGBT faculty and lodging complaints about 'bias' in the classroom.

The Brit, Milo Yiannopolous, darling of the right, gay, married to a black man, out and loud, has been banned from a myriad of campuses because students are offended by his views. I believe they are offended by him because they have been told to be offended by him because he's a libertarian conservative.

I would suggest that the US promotes the value of free expression, reminding the opposition of your First Amendment. Intellectual diversity is good, anything else is bad.

What about the supposedly sensible people at the World Health Organisation?

The World Health Organisation has recently removed a page from its website explaining the difference between sex and gender. It described how women menstruate and men have testicles. Now biological sex is an inconvenient truth for the gender neutral mob. This is simple science. As Germanine Greer said, just because you cut off your penis, that doesn't make you female.

WHO's website and policy goals have been re-written at vast expense to take into consideration the new brave world of gender determined by non binary people.

Back in the UK – transport gender segregation is mooted by leading socialists (who else?)

A socialist MP Chris Williamson has floated the idea of "women only" carriages on trains to combat sexual assault in what is a flagrant attempt at gender segregation.

The London Evening Standard reports that there were 6,057 violent and sexual offences on the capital's railways, tube trains and stations in 2016, compared to 5,137 the year before.

The MP looked at the number of sexual assaults and thought banning men from certain carriages could be the answer.

This is downright offensive towards the majority of men who would never dream of sexually assaulting a woman. It's also an admittance that the authorities are giving up on trying to prosecute assaults.

Williamson said: "It would be worth consulting about it. It was pooh-poohed [when Jeremy Corbyn, Marxist leader of UK Labour party suggested it], but the statistics seem to indicate there is some merit in examining that.

"Complemented with having more guards on trains, it would be a way of combating these attacks, which have seen a very worrying increase in the past few years.

"I'm not saying it has to happen, but it may create a safe space. It would be a matter of personal choice whether someone wanted to make use of it."

These men really don't understand. In their desperate attempts to feminise themselves they do not recognise that this doesn't keep women safe to restrict their movements – it normalises attacks. The attackers and their over active penises are the problem, not women's travel.

The level of discrimination against both men and women is absolutely sickening – gender segregation would be a backward step for Britain. Maybe the man who suggested it should sit in his own carriage, far away from everyone else… or would these feminazi men have us wearing burkas? Or, to take it to its extreme, would they propose segregating ethnic minorities to shield them from possible racism?

President Trump's enlightened policy on banning transgenders from the military – commonsense or prejudice?

I love Donald, I even campaigned for him during his election and was in Trump Tower on election night, but is he right to ban transgenders from the military?

I believe President Trump was right to ban transgender surgery for serving military personnel, after all, why should the taxpayers pay for their sexuality of choice?

When President Obama repealed the ban that transgenders could not openly serve in the military I do not suppose for one minute, in his politically correct little mind, he thought of the unintended consequences.

Trump initially banned transgender people from serving in the US military. That ban was overturned by federal judges who said 'it was probably unconstitutional'. The ban is now being re-assessed as to whether transgenders are capable of deployment 'except under certain circumstances'. Given the mental health issues associated with transgenders, I think this is a legitimate call. Lives are at risk on the frontline and if you suffer from mental anguish of any kind – transgender or otherwise – then a professional psychiatric assessment should be made of your ability to serve.

Trump has made the right call.

He is not alone. There are few countries that allow transgenders to serve in their militaries. The EU is not so open and inclusive on this subject.

Gender neutralising our schools

The UK's Good Schools Guide is to examine how 'transgender-friendly' schools are in future, praising 'fabulous efforts' by some institutions.

Stating that the issue had been 'building up' over the last 18 months. Eighteen months - that is a mere micro second in human development. The Guide's spokesman said kids are suffering undue stress at schools which neglect to use the name or pronoun they prefer, or to wear a uniform and use facilities for the gender they identify with.

Now they are now going to mention in their guide whether the schools are making 'fabulous efforts' in the transgender arena.

And then we learn that 'Educate and Celebrate' an officially funded website by the UK's Department for Education, which is an extremist site for LGBT activists, is pushing an LGBT programme where boys and girls' uniforms are abandoned and material promoting gay and transgender lifestyles is inserted into every facet of school life.

At least 150 schools have signed up to display this 'charity's' wares in reception areas, assemblies and all lessons. For little tots aged between five and seven they have provided a helpful geography lesson with penguins – two male penguins who adopt a baby penguin, entitled 'Penguin Habitats' which will, according to the lunatics, 'challenge typical behaviour and gender stereotyping' and 'actively confront prejudice'.

Again, I question where has the authority for this come from? Why are we allowing an extreme group of a tiny minority asking silly questions for which those who are supposed to be educating kids pander to? Parents who cannot control their children's internet searching and severe pandering to kids with over active imaginations. And schools which should be a safe space for learning are confronted in the reception area and throughout our school curriculums on very marginal issues. The people in charge of our children's safeguarding and welfare are jumping to the feminazi's tune fearing that if they do not produce a policy, a space on the website, re-think uniforms and toilet arrangements, they are somehow phobic.

Private schools opt-outs

Private schools have fought back but I have mis-givings about the schools that have won the right to opt out of LGBT teaching. According to the Sunday Times, children will no longer be taught about gay marriage, cohabiting couples or same-sex families.

While there is no choice in state funded schools whether they have LGBT issues taught, at least the private sector is fighting back.

Many independent faith schools have refused to teach a LGBT curriculum. A Jewish boys school put stickers over images in books of women in short-sleeved dresses. It also refused to teach that some people were different because of sexual orientation or gender reassignment.

One school in Leicester taught boys it was acceptable for husbands to beat their wives, Muslim I would have thought?

I may not agree with some of their regressive teachings, but at least those who shout loudest in the name of faith, private money or lobbying, have the option to opt out. So should all parents, whether they can afford private school fees or not.

The Islamisation of our state schools

In the meantime, whilst the libs are running the mental asylum, Islam is creeping up behind and biting us faster than we can stop it. In UK schools we now have girls as young as five wearing the hijab. In church schools up and down the country, young Muslim girls are being sexualised by being forced to wear a headscarf. Normally, Muslim girls are not required to wear a hijab until puberty. But in the 'right-on' UK, these poor little cherubs are being subjected to hiding their hair under a scarf from the age of five.

I feel so strongly about this issue, so much so that when in September 2018 Marks and Spencer started selling hijabs for young girls, much to a media outrage, I wrote to the chairman as follows:

Mr Archie Norman
Chairman
Marks and Spencer plc
Waterside House
35 North Wharf Road
London W2 1NW

Dear Mr Norman

I recently sent you a letter in which I voiced my objections to M&S selling hijab's for young girls. In response, your executive team pointed out that "a number of schools requested the option of a hijab", and that M&S consequently "responded to this demand".

Based on the answer I received I have to conclude that M&S does not quite appreciate what is at stake. Since M&S is not operating in the vacuum of the market, the 'demand principle' alone can never justify selling hijabs for children. Your company's policies and the products it sells have an impact that goes beyond the mere transaction between you and your customers. Your policies and products have a societal impact as well, and M&S has a responsibility here.

Applying the logic used by your colleague to a similar case, would it really be sensible for M&S to start selling sexy underwear for children if there would be a demand for this? Or, to use another extreme example, would M&S consider selling clothes carrying Nazi-style insignia? Now you may reply that there is no such demand and thus you don't sell any of the above. Nevertheless, even in case there would be such demand, I doubt M&S would make these types of products available to its customers. And for good reason.

Indeed, running a company like M&S means you have a corporate responsibility. The impact of your decision to sell hijab products for young girls has effects that go way beyond responding to a certain demand. Providing certain garments may be lucrative for M&S in the short run, but this does not absolve M&S from following ethical standards.

Surely, you have enough empathy to appreciate the potential adverse effects it may have on the development of small girls when they are dressed up in M&S hijabs? To be clear, the use of hijabs by women is not a religious requirement. In fact, there is no Koranic requirement at all for women to wear a hijab, and certainly not for young Muslim girls. By selling hijabs to children, M&S effectively facilitates the spread of an extreme version of Islam. This issue has a human rights dimension to it, and involves the rights of children in particular. Are you aware that recently when some primary schools removed the need for hijabs there was a backlash from the hardline men from the mosques and the male parent/teacher governors to have them reimposed? Do you know that there are many brave women around the world living in oppressive Islamic regimes who are trying to rid themselves of this misogynistic garment and are being jailed or worse, stoned to death for their stance against radicalism? Moreover, by selling these products now, you do not merely serve customers today, but will likely fuel further demand which will lead Britain into an apartheid of those who do not wear hijabs, to the poor little girls who are made to wear them.

I am sure M&S operates according to the various equality acts that are in place. Can you honestly say that you approve of segregating little girls, hiding their hair which, in all probability, will lead to them being forced to wearing the burqa. Please take a look around some of our cities - Tower Hamlets is a short distance from M&S HQ - I would be happy to accompany you, to see what is taking place in the UK.

M&S cannot continue to ignore the wider societal consequences of its company policies. Therefore, in the interests of the wellbeing of the children involved, British society, as well as your company, I urge M&S to reconsider its decision to sell hijabs to young girls as indeed John Lewis did.

Yours, etc

The reply from the chairman's 'executive office' was thus:

"We recognise that this garment provokes strong reactions from different customers, but it is not for M&S to have a view on what people should or shouldn't wear as this is a personal decision for individuals and parents.

"We provide bespoke uniforms for 250 schools across the country and they tell us which items they need as part of their school uniform list. For a number of schools this year, they requested the option of the hijab."

M&S are still selling hijabs.

The arguments (from the libs) is 'what if they want to be just like mum?'. My reply is, does that apply to the women who were too short skirts, high heels, red lipstick, and so on?

This is the libs caving in because of the fear of being called an Islamophobe. We live in a Western secular country, mainly influenced by the Christian faith. This Saudi-sexualisation of young girls should be resisted at all costs. However, I fear we will lose the battle if we gender neutralise our children.

UK family to sue Church of England school over boys in dresses

A Christian family is threatening to sue their six-year-old son's school because a boy in his class is allowed to wear a dress.

Shockingly, the parents took the decision to remove both sons from the school and to home school them. They took this decision for an older sibling, 8 years, because a boy in his class started wearing a dress.

The parents complained that the school was not taking their views as Christians – in a Christian school – into account. They said their son was confused because the boy in dresses sometimes dressed as a boy and sometimes as a girl.

The parents are very generous Christians and invited the trans child to their son's birthday party, the theme being 'royal'. Most boys turned up as knights but the trans child wore a blue velvet dress.

They take an active role in the school and have stated that as Christians gender dysphoria is something they need to address with love and compassion, but not in the sphere of a primary school. (They are better people than me).

I think the school, church and local council have got it totally wrong and out of perspective. Instead of supporting the majority view and these Christian parents, they are taking an extremist view in quoting the 2010 Equality Act when, in reality, under the Equality Act gender reassignment only applies to people over the age of 18.

I also think that the school is discriminating against the couple by implying that the couple are transphobic because they wish to bring up their sons with regard to the Christian faith. One of the saddest parts of this story is that the parents feel they have to resort to law as the defenders of their faith have let them down. The Archbishop of Canterbury, supposed defender of the worldwide Anglican church cannot be relied upon to uphold the beliefs of his Christian flock. He too is often at odds with the fellowship across the US and Africa.

School classrooms should be safe environments for children and Christian schools should be defending Christian values and the rule of law. Instead, this new trans ideology is being aggressively imposed on schools, parents and children. Our schools are becoming a battlefield of dangerous ideology with vulnerable children being used and abused by radical militants.

If any child should be withdrawn from school it is the little lad dressing up in dresses on the days he feels like it as this poor little tot needs help and quickly.

The feminizas and right-on warriors, not content with waging gender wars in our boardrooms and bathrooms, now turn their warped world to targeting children.

The attempts to make schools gender neutral is their next battle which, if we do not fight back, they will win.

They are taught to see gender as a problem to be discussed and solved. A small number of adults are taking charge of what our children should think – from climate change, to obesity, to world output and unfairness of GDP and capitalism. They are taught that gender is not down to biology but feelings and social convention. Those that do not believe in the gender wars for religious beliefs are bigots and quite mad. It is often said that cultures and civilisations die because they are attacked from within, not from those outside.

What happens when Christians refuse to accommodate gay or trans people?

I have stated before that I have no faith. I grew up in the bosom of the Church of England, being educated at a church school, sent to Sunday school and I joined the Church run Girls' Brigade (distinct from the boys), but I absolutely defend Christian rights in our Western Christian dominant cultures.

There have been a few cases of Christians being persecuted in the UK.

When a Christian printer refused to print stationery for a transgender person it hit the headlines. The trans person is outraged, thinks it is chilling and unnecessary.

When a couple running a small hotel refused to let a room to a gay couple – they were taken to court and criminalized.

Then there were the Christian bakers who refused to bake a cake for a gay campaign. They were criminalized. The 'Equality Commission' said when the bakers lost through the Court of Appeal: "The judgement today was very clear. It said unequivocally, faith is important, but faith cannot set aside equality legislation that has been long fought."

A lawyer who worked on some of these cases made the point that these rulings could force Muslim printers to produce materials with the Prophet Mohammed, which is forbidden under the Koran. Similarily, if a gay printer refused to print a Muslim message saying gay marriages are a sin or that all gays should be stoned or killed, that would be against the law.

Luckily, on appeal, common sense prevailed and it was recognised that the couple were not wrong to stick to their faith. Although I cannot help wondering whether this decision was made because the couple come from religiously divided Northern Ireland and that the ruling took into consideration the potential persecution of Muslims over the same issue.

Yet in a free society are we not covered by our beliefs and morals? If that is taken away by modern laws that do not adhere to thousands of years of doctrine, where does that leave us as human beings? This is a one-way street with a chilling deadly end.

And when gender nonsense goes wrong in prisons – a convicted rapist, now identifying as a woman, still with a penis, attacks women in prison

When you think it can't get any worse, this story comes along.

Joseph, a father-of-three, who became Jilly behind bars, was moved from a male only prison to a female prison.

Double rapist Joseph, who had a £10,000 sex change operation behind bars, has been put into segregation after making unwanted sexual advances on women prisoners – she/he/it, still has a penis.

In 2009 following a High Court ruling, transgender prisoners were allowed to transfer to different sex jails.

Joseph, with his penis, is the result of the law of unintended consequences. The law is an ass and the female inmates are paying for Joseph's penis.

There are numerous stories such as this. The State sends criminals to prison. Then the taxpayers are forced to pay for their sexual perversions by changing sex. Are we then surprised that the men living as 'women' are attacked by other men?

Whilst there cannot ever be justification for violence, prison is a violent place, inhabited by violent criminals. The answer isn't moving these mentally unstable perverts to a female prison, it's not allowing them to indulge their fantasies and illness on the taxpayers.

There are men living as women in category A prisons – prisons that house the most dangerous criminals in the UK. They include Islamist jihadis. I wonder what the tolerant jihadis make of these poor creatures? And I do wonder whether they would be charged for violence against trannies? I doubt it.

To place a rapist among women because he claims to be a woman, at an horrendous cost to the UK taxpayers, might be the act of the psychotics who are now in charge of our prisons? The cult of gender fluidity just got more dangerous.

Women in prison deserve to be kept safe, whatever their crimes committed. To put him in the same space as vulnerable women is putting his minority narcissistic self identity trump over the rights of real women. It puts their security at risk, his fantasy takes precedence over these women's rights.

The liberal left media are not horrified for the women prisoners at risk of this transgender rapist, but because right thinking journalists used the term 'transgender rapist'.

It gets worse. Some left/lib pro-trans gender activists/observers have now slammed the media for 'dead naming' the twice convicted criminal for using the factual information that this man committed two rapes. It is sickening that they would like to erase the fact that this man was a rapist, it doesn't matter that he now thinks of himself as Jessica, he is still a violent convicted rapist, with a penis.

The notorious and evil child killer Ian Huntley now identifies as a woman. He is a danger whether he is a man or a woman. He should stay in a male category A prison.

And the people behind the activists and change in law?

Never far from any campaign against conservatism is George Soros. Whatever 'rights' is the flavour of the year/decade, his cash is behind it, or rather his front organisation, Open Europe. And the gender agenda is no different.

He helpfully funded a European report 'Legal Gender Recognition in Europe, toolkit'. https://www.tgeu.org/sites/default/files/Toolkit_web.pdf

Our Justice system is being abused

The extremists in the trans world are prosecuting anyone who disagree with them through the UK courts.

Linda Bellos, a far left, black, Jewish, feminist lesbian is facing a trial because she told an audience at a rally for the Gender Reconciliation Act that she would, "…thump any trans activists that came near her."

She was reported to the police, the matter was dropped but the trans activist, Giuliana Kendal, an openly transgender woman, took out a private prosecution against Bellos.

Bellos established Black History Month in the UK, was elected to run a major London local authority and is, to say the least, 'radical and progressive', completely right-on and certainly not a conservative.

She was invited to speak at Cambridge University on trans politics and alerted the organisers that she would question, "some of the trans politics … which seems to assert the power of those who were previously designated male to tell lesbians, and especially lesbian feminists, what to say and what to think". She was no-platformed, the invitation cancelled, because "the welfare of the students in this instance has to come first".

Cambridge is one of the world's top universities and state funded. Why is this being allowed to happen?

Quite simply because no one is challenging them and when they do, even from the Left, they are attacked physically, on social media or via the justice system.

Politicians are afraid to openly discuss this phenomenon for fear of attack and they don't like to be labelled 'phobic'. A few writers are now starting to voice their concerns, but in a very softly softly way so as not to offend. That will not work, they are just swept aside as an irritant and the mission creeps ever further into our state funded institutions.

The no-platforming and safe spaces agenda is a whole new book.

TV programme Father Ted co-creator Graham Linehan has been given a police harassment warning after transgender activist Stephanie Hayden reported him for addressing her as "he" rather than as "her", and for using her former male names.

It's now a crime to say 'women don't have penises'

Is it now a crime to tell the truth in Britain? It's heading that way. Merseyside Police are making 'enquiries' into a trans-sceptical group that distributed stickers saying 'Women don't have penises'. Yes, that's right: the police, the actual police, are investigating a group for expressing what the vast majority of people consider to be a biological, social, actual fact: that if you have a penis you are not a female. What next: arrest people for saying the sky is blue or that unicorns aren't real?

A trans extremist campaigner promised that he would get the police to 'identify those responsible' for these outrageous declarations of scientific truth. These sticker heretics are an affront to Liverpool's history of 'diversity' and 'equality', he said. A fancy way of saying they are 'thought criminals'. And lo, the Merseyside Police duly got involved: 'We are aware of this matter and enquiries are being made.'

Consider what is being done here. Not only are the police making enquiries about the expression of an idea, which is something they should never do; but even worse, they are making enquiries about speech that simply said, 'Women do not have penises'. That is true. If you have a penis, you are male. If you have a vagina, you are female. Of course, people with penises should be at liberty to call themselves women and change their names and so on – but that doesn't mean the rest of us have to accept that they really are women. They clearly are not.

How has it become so controversial to say this? Because the atmosphere around trans issues has become alarmingly so. Everything from saying 'Women don't have penises' to having a Hollywood actress star in a film about a trans man is now branded 'transphobia'.

Feminists who meet to discuss the Gender Recognition Act and the fact that it will allow almost anyone to identify as a woman are harassed, censored, and in some cases physically attacked. Woe betide anyone who turns up to a campus to raise questions about the transgender ideology: they can expect by the moral guardians who govern student politics.

Misogyny as a hate crime

I have concentrated on the lunacy of conservatives joining the #MeToo brigade because we are fully aware of the lunatic Left's winning crusade in all areas covered by this book.

My fear is that we are too late to do anything to reverse this madness as our institutions are so infected and too far down the line in not just accepting but implementing laws to interpret a very small minorities perceptions of hate.

For example, a socialist MP is bringing forward a bill for misogyny to become a hate crime. She seems to have the full support of our polices forces, backed up by wimmin's groups, such as the Fawcett Society. The Fawcett Society is a bunch of highly educated women, supported with a fat endowment, The Government Equalities Office (taxpayers' cash), and Comic Relief, amongst others which enables them to have a loud voice at the tables of lawmaking and influence.

They recently gave 'evidence' in Parliament about this proposed law:

Recording misogyny hate crime

"Hate crime against women and girls is a cause and consequence of gender inequality and should be treated as unlawful", they say.

"It is important that the hate crime in question is misogyny hate crime, not gender hate crime, recognising the direction of the power imbalance within society and the reality of the endemic scale of violence against women and girls. This is consistent with the one-directional nature within law of for example, hate crime committed against disabled people or on the basis of transgender identity". Really?

The recording of hate crime incidents against women and girls has already begun in some police forces. Nottinghamshire Police have worked with the Nottingham Women's Centre to implement the recording of misogyny hate crime and hate incidents, as part of a strategy to tackle misogyny. The police began to recognise misogyny as a hate crime on the 4_{th} April 2016. They define misogyny hate crime as follows:

Misogyny hate crime may be understood as incidents against women that are motivated by the attitude of men towards women and includes behaviour targeted at women by men simply because they are women. Examples of this may include unwanted or uninvited sexual advances; physical or verbal assault; unwanted or uninvited physical or verbal contact or engagement; use of mobile devices to send unwanted or uninvited messages or take photographs without consent or permission. Domestic abuse is not included within the scope of Misogyny hate crime in this procedure as it is dealt with comprehensively within its own procedure.

The hate element of the incident or crime constitutes a flag or "qualifier" on the incident log, but does not change the offence or incident itself. This change was accompanied by training for all police staff, carried out by the Women's Centre.

The intention of recording incidents in this way is that the police will be able to raise awareness of the seriousness of these incidences and encourage women to report them. This will enable them to gather better intelligence, to disrupt activities and perpetrators, improve risk management and support the women affected. The long-term aim is to nudge people towards a culture shift and to reframe misogynist behaviour as socially undesirable.

Media reports in December 2017 stated that Nottinghamshire police had received 153 reports of misogynistic hate incidents, of which 61 were classified as a crime and dealt with accordingly.[1]

North Yorkshire police have now also followed Nottinghamshire's lead, Avon and Somerset have plans in place to do so[2] and other police forces are considering following suit. The National Police Chiefs' Council are considering how to take forward this trend

The problem I have with these polices forces adopting this minority agenda, is that they have taken the views of a small minority, highly motivated, men hating, Left agenda.

---

1   https://www.nottinghampost.com/news/local-news/more-150-men-reported-police-1073822
2   ITV News. (2017). *Avon & Somerset Police to officially recognise gender-based hate as a crime.* http://www.itv.com/news/westcountry/2017-10-16/avon-somerset-police-to-officially-recognise-gender-based-hate-as-a-crime/

In the UK, our police forces have lost 44,000 police and staff over the past few years. Yet, they are required to examine so called hate crime, such as 'misogyny'. Now senior police women have hit back.

Sara Thornton of the National Police Chiefs Council hit back recently and said that it wasn't and couldn't be a priority to look into such 'crimes'. With exponentially rising violent crime something had to give. She said they were not going to investigate reports of misogyny by dead people.

The next day, the UK's most senior police officer, Cressida Dick, head of London's Metropolitan Police, agreed with Thornton.

Of course, there will be politics behind these women's statements. Dick is usually politically correct. I would also take it as a pinch of salt that two women are speaking out on this issue. Their real message is police cuts, presided over by a Conservative government.

Mrs Thatcher knew that to keep the public onside and to keep us safe, the armed forces and our police were top priorities for manpower and funding.

The Left is particularly loud and again well-funded in promoting imagined 'misogyny crime' and our stupid governments have pandered to them.

It is now time to re-evaluate our priorities – dead stabbed children, drug crime, burglary and murder – or, appeasing a few women hurt by tweets or wolf whistles.

Extremists use the university system to target and harass normal thinking and their own colleagues

The loudest and most active of the transactivists are sitting in our universities, paid for by the taxpayers. They are at the root of the violent TERF movement and the bullying of anyone who does not agree with their warped views, including women in their own universities.

Transactivist Natacha Kennedy (aka as Mark Hellen) heads up a blacklist of academics who challenge the view that biological men can be women. She is on the payroll at Goldsmiths University, London.

These people inhabit a closed Facebook group and provides 'targets' for trans activists accusing academics of 'hate speech' if they question whether a man can identify as a woman and vice versa.

They school them into how to file hate crime reports to their universities, the police and how to target them at work.

The women's battle of our borders – migrants, sexual harassment and rapes

Where are the feminazis, standing up for the European females that have been sexually assaulted, abused and raped by the millions of marauding migrants let into our continent?

No one asked us if we minded accommodating thousands of young sexually oppressed, misogynistic, illiterate men from the Middle East and Africa.

They poured into our continent looking for a better life, few (10%) were from war torn countries and therefore real refugees. As economic migrants, they saw it as their right to march into our towns and cities, demanding work, housing and benefits. But they took much more, they abused our women.

Yet, the feminazi left, aided by the charities, NGOs, the UN, the EU, the alt-left and the liberals, they came in their millions.

There was a quiet war going on in our towns and cities that went unreported. Women were being assaulted, raped and the authorities were turning a blind eye. From the police, the politicians and our media. Across Sweden, Germany, Austria, Norway, Finland and the EU there was a blanket wall of silence. Thankfully, social media forced this onto the agenda.

Since 2015 Sweden has taken the highest number of migrants. On New Years' Eve 2015/16 reports of hundreds of youths from Afghanistan roamed the streets in Malmo and surrounded intoxicated girls/women and harassed them. Similar reports came in from other migrant heavy towns. Finland reported the same.

Swedish lawyer, Elisabeth Fritz, claims the majority of rape cases she has had to work on the suspects have all been from migrant backgrounds. However, her claims have been called into question because liberal Sweden does not gather statistics on migrant crime. The police are slowly confirming that this is happening. If we do not record, call those who blow the whistle – or even speak the truth – perpetrators of hate crime, how can we deal with the crimes against women?

And Sweden's response? It has now issued a handbook to help teenage migrants about sex, consent and gender. They cite 'culture clashes' and to know their rights and responsibilities now they are in Sweden.

It is no wonder that the Swedish Democrats, a party that campaigns to protects its borders and culture, is close to power in Sweden.

There are 'no go zones' in many towns, with Malmo becoming the rape capital of Europe. With murders, shootings, rapes and robberies – all came with the arrival of Middle Eastern and African migrants.

Failure to report from our authorities has led to a cover-up, little debate because of a fear of being called racist, xenophobic or hateful which leads the liberal left into a quandary on how to deal with such unprecedented attacks on our women.

A director of events at Stockholm City Council said he had been utterly unaware of the risk of such attacks:

'It was a modus operandi that we had never seen before: large groups of young men who surround girls and molest them.'

There are too many incidents to list across the EU but I will recall the problems in Germany when Frau Merkel opened the floodgates where there were instances of rape and assault that were equally shocking.

In 2015 Merkel made the biggest mistake of her life – and ours – she opened Germany's borders to over 1 million 'refugees'.

Again, on that same New Year's Eve of 2105/16, Merkel opened her borders to sexual offences, rapes and harassment of Germany's women in Cologne, Stuttgart, Hamburg and Munich. In Cologne as many as 1,000 men of Arab and North African origin formed rings around women, who tried to fight their way out. On January 1st, Cologne police issued a statement to say that celebrations had gone 'peacefully', not mentioning the 500 criminal complaints, with fifty per cent involving allegations of sexual offences. Yet, a secret police report said they were overwhelmed by the attacks and crime, there were simply too many at the same time.

Social media was soon on the case. Were the police and authorities repentant with apologies and the truth? No, even the female Mayor of Cologne suggested that the attacks were the fault of the women and proposed a code of conduct - for the women – not the men.

Merkel's hold on government was, thankfully, loosened in 2017 when the Germans went to the polls and elected a pro-nation state and anti-immigrant party, women such as the AfD's Beatrice Von Storch and Alice Weidel (a lesbian). The AfD gained 90 seats in the Bundestag. Good luck to them. It is the women of the right who will protect our liberties which were hard fought for.

It's not the battle of the boardrooms, sexism, transgender rights and working women that are our new problems, it's our battle to keep our hard fought rights against the backdrop of open borders, illegal immigrant invasions where we have let people in who have no idea of democracy, human rights, women's rights and fairness.

Sexual grooming gangs in Britain

For decades UK Pakistani men have been raping and grooming white working class girls. The authorities from social workers, the police and politicians all turned a blind eye. It was an inconvenient truth that was not allowed to be discussed because of multiculturalism and the fear of being branded racist.

It is estimated that up to a million girls (and boys) could be affected.

Fortunately, those men are now being identified and convicted.

There is less outrage about the children and young people who have been abused and more about the language used to describe these paedophiles. Whether 'Asian' is the correct term? Does that then vilify a whole continent? Or does the tag 'Pakistani' mean the whole of Pakistan?

This makes me so angry. Let's call it what it is. They are first, second and third generation Pakistani Muslim men that have never been challenged about their way of life. The discussion on terminology is a distraction and demeaning and damaging to the girls, some of whom are now women. It's the women that matter, not the men.

Ban on Boobs - Group think on our transport system

UK: The Advertising Standards Authority decided that it will ban advertisements which 'reinforce harmful gender stereotypes', such as women using soft soap or little girls dreaming of being ballerinas.

The argument is not whether stereotypes are harmful but a tacit agreement but only those unelected quangos at the ASA - a regulatory body, not an elected one - but what right does it think it has to occupy this political space? They formerly used a test for adverts: was an ad legal, decent and truthful? Now it seeks to turn the industry into a tool for promoting its version of how they see UK society should act.

Our diminutive London Mayor, Sadiq Khan, or 'Khan't' as we know him, decided a year ago to ban 'body shaming' ads for a weight loss brand. A very attractive bikini clad woman asked 'Are you Beach Ready'? Well, I don't know about you, but my body certainly isn't beach ready and I welcome any chance to reduce its horrid size.

Mr Khan't, in the name of political correctness, the obese who feel ashamed and the feminazis, flexed his toned muscles and told us that we could no longer see these images and so banned them. He also felt that they portrayed an unhealthy or unrealistic look. I think obese people are unhealthy but it seems it's ok for them to be shielded so they can stuff their faces with fat and sugar.

Some argue that it wasn't about body shaming but that it was his Muslim faith and fellow followers who were offended.

In 1994, supermodel Eva Herzigova, launched the Wonderbra, with one of the most successful advertising campaigns ever launched. Motorists in Trafalfar Square caused traffic jams and bumped cars whilst oggling at the advert.

This underwear certainly 'enabled' women with the push up bra, well it certainly did for me as I'm still wearing this wonderful uplifting garment. Despite complaints from feminazis, it has been one of the most successful undergarments ever sold.

In October 2017 the hosiery company wanted to use this image to promote its new panty hose but the bosses of Transport for London (tubes and busses, boss of which is Mayor Sadiq Kahn), asked the 'offending' backless model to be covered up – with a 'boob tube' - as they objected to a topless model.

There was not a boob in sight, only a very nice back and a bottom through opaque tights. This is graceful, beautiful and fun. What on earth is wrong with it?

What is wrong is the attitude of a group of officious, pompous pen pushers who think they are safe-guarding our moralities and sensitivities.

Why would ordinary woman on the London public transport system object to this? The only 'people' objecting are the official keepers of dangerous, patronising politically correct, morality policing group think and the narrow minded bigots who object to women's bodies that women do not want or need.

NHS

The beloved NHS is strapped for cash, apparently, yet I have to question how they spend our money.

Some years ago I had a meeting with a chief executive of a health trust (the body that decides how our taxpayer cash is spent within the NHS). This woman, wearing a crucifix (when it was allowed – religious symbols are banned, except for, of course Muslim headscarves) told me with a completely straight face, that she was restricting the number of cycles a woman could have on the NHS for fertility/invitro treatment. Anyone that has undergone this heart rendering procedure – the cost in terms of cash and human heartache – will know that one cycle is useless and needs at least three cycles for it to have a chance of being viable. Yet, she proudly announced that transgender operations will be carried out on the NHS, because 'there is a need'.

So, the 'need' needs funding:

An excerpt from a liberal Left newspaper: *In 2015-16, the NHS in England put an additional £4.4m towards funding gender identity services and have set aside additional funding for 2016-17 of about £3m to the adult clinics and £2.2m for the Tavistock clinic.*

Will Huxter, the chair of the NHS England gender task and finish group, said: "We're keen to get waiting times down as quickly as we possibly can."

Experts agree that the key obstacle to reducing waiting times, apart from lack of funding, is getting appropriately trained staff to fill posts in gender identity clinics. You can throw all the money you want at a service, but unless you have people who are trained and skilled to work in those areas, you're not going to improve capacity.

Huxter agrees and says part of the problem is that there isn't a specialised training strand that sees medical professionals emerge from training ready to work in the gender identity clinics. "We

are working with Health Education England and the GMC [General Medical Council] about how we could improve that for the future," he said.
https://www.theguardian.com/society/2016/jul/10/transgender-clinic-waiting-times-patient-numbers-soar-gender-identity-services

Will Huxter, is 'the chair of the NHS England gender task and finish group' – does anyone else think that this guy sounds like he's offering a cut and blow dry?

We are a country that cannot look after it's elderly, calling them 'NHS bedblockers' when they cannot be discharged from hospital, although they are recovered from a serious illness because we do not have enough day care or nursing home facilities. Instead, where we have too few nurses and midwives and import our GPs and surgeons from third world countries, leaving those countries in a worst health state because of our failure to train our own health professionals, or we are the 'go to' health tourist destination for Nigeria women to give birth, or that uncontrolled migration brought new diseases and resurrected diseases we had eradicated and using GP and hospital facilities that are under resourced and not planned for. Instead, we indulge in transgender Frankenstein operations, mutilating bodies, rather than giving life and joy to ordinary couples who desperately want a child or allowing our elderly and sick to die in dignity.

A General Practitioner gave a 12-year-old, sex change drugs

You would expect private clinics to get involved in what must be quite a lucrative business. There are always those out to make a quick buck from other people's misery and the trans industry is no different. Free enterprise capitalism is great, but too often it preys on the cash rich vulnerable.

A female UK doctor is being investigated by a regulatory body after complaints from two NHS consultants which imposed an order to stop her from treating trans patients unsupervised.

Working from her home, she treats people wishing to change sex. She offers her services to children who had been denied sex change treatments on the NHS. She had given cross-sex hormones to four child patients, one of whom is only 12-years-old.

This woman has been practising on vulnerable children and giving serious life-changing treatment to children who are too young to know what they are doing. The long-term effects, particularly on girls – who are left with irreversible effects – is tragic.

These children should be offered counselling, never drugs. Children's identities are fluid, often confused and unable to take life-changing and life-threatening decisions at a young and vulnerable age. The parents also need counselling in proper parenting.

I predict a huge backlash once some of these children become adults, when they reach 21 years of age (the time when most people have reached full bodily and mental maturity). They will start suing their parents (particularly in the US with its compensation culture, and increasingly in the UK which is following suit) and the gender industry for mutilating them, messing with their minds and not just referring them to counselling where they might have grown out of this current fad. (See chapter 12, John)

Our state funded broadcasters

Channel 4, a UK publicly funded (by guarantee), very leftist organisation that has embraced gender neutral toilets, but not everyone is happy.

They have come under considerable criticism and something which I agree with. Those having to endure same sex toilets have complained:

Men leave the toilet seats up – women don't.

Men pee around the bowl and on the floor.

Women leave used sanitary products in and around the bins provided.

These are just a few of the objections, there are more in this book.

Channel 4's weekly, nightly hour long news programme is something to behold. A hot bed of Marxism, night after night pours into our homes. It's main anchorman, Jon Snow, was recently filmed at the Glastonbury music event singing 'Fuck the Tories'. He has subsequently denied this, claiming he is impartial.

His fellow presenter, Cathy Newman, recently had a run in with Jordan Peterson, the Canadian philosopher. It really is something to behold and I suggest you Google it.

The BBC, which used to be trusted and the place to go for breaking news and commentary, is no longer trusted.

They are obsessed with gender and identity politics. Whether it is race, colour, religion, quotas, gender, transgender, the BBC is the main promoter of divisive politics.

So much so, that their morning political flagship programme on BBC Radio 4, *Today*, has lost 1m listeners in a year.

Their main opposition agenda: Brexit, Trump, men, conservatism, white people, controlling our borders, capitalism, populism, low taxes, any right wing think tank and people that hate the UK and traditional values. Any invited guest gets a hard time, an inquisition with sneering questioning, particularly from the gender quota, Mishal Hussein.

Their main topics for discussion, where the interviewees are given carte blanche and reverence: Hillary Clinton, anyone who hates the UK, anti Brexiteers, Trump haters, uncontrolled immigration, open borders and critics of Israel. You can hear the interviewers' reverent tones, you can hear the smiles in their voices and their overt complicity with the opposition agenda. Their promoter in chief is Justin Webb, former US correspondent.

Their White House editor, Jon Sopel, is an embarrassing spectacle with his overt hatred of Trump and Republicanism and love for Obama and the Clintons. I suggest the BBC retires him soon before he makes himself ill.

However, our national treasure, John Humphreys, tries to keep a neutral tone.

The programme has gone down hill since Sarah Sands took up the editorship. Although I am sure the tentacles at the top of the BBC have a hand in this agenda too.

Chapter 3

Gender - How do you 'Self Identify'? (the current buzz phrase)

What is self-identification?

To believe that you are a particular kind of person, especially when other people do not think that you are that kind of person: Cambridge Dictionary

Which is a bit tricky. It's like being a conservative or a populist, depending on one's view, you are either an extremist or just right. Or you support one football team rather than another, or are you a cat or dog person?

But sex is altogether different. You are the sex you were born into.

However, politicians and extreme lobby groups see it differently. In the mad house that I currently inhabit – that venerable institution of intolerance, the alt-left and the lunatics – the European Union, has produced a handy guide to how you self-identify. This is also enshrined in legislation.

Normal people would think that you could only be a man or a woman, you may feel you have to identify according to your politics, but not the EU. They have produced a handy guide to explain the 'working definitions' of gender:

The acronym **LGBTI** describes a diverse group of persons who do not conform to conventional or traditional notions of male and female gender roles. LGBTI people are also sometimes referred to as "sexual, gender and bodily minorities".

A **lesbian** is a woman whose enduring physical, romantic and/or emotional attraction is to other women.

Gay is often used to describe a man whose enduring physical, romantic and/or emotional attraction is to other men, although the term can be used to describe both gay men and lesbians.

Bisexual describes an individual who is physically, romantically and/or emotionally attracted to both men and women.

Transgender describes people whose gender identity and/or gender expression differs from the sex they were assigned at birth.

The term **intersex** covers bodily variations in regard to culturally established standards of maleness and femaleness, including variations at thelevel of chromosomes, gonads and genitals.

Sexual orientation refers to each person's capacity for emotional, affective and sexual attraction to, and intimate and sexual relations with, individuals of a different or the same gender or more than one gender.

Gender identity refers to each person's deeply felt internal and individual experience of gender, which may or may not correspond with the sex assigned at birth.

Then there is the whole new, complicated and confusing gender terms:

The lunatics, having taken over the asylum have produced a whole new lexicon of words to confuse normal people.

Gone are the titles and pronouns: Mr, Mrs, Ms (do you remember when Ms was controversial and a little bit edgy?), he, she, him, her.

They now wish us to refer to this tiny minority by their pronouns. If we do not comply we can be convicted of 'hate crime'.

A handy guide:

Cis – is the pronoun you use as the gender you were born with. Then there are those who confuse everyone by having the 'right' to be addressed with the following pronouns:

ze, hir, zir, xe, xem, xyr

Apparently, according to a handy guide: 'Respecting a person's pronouns is vitally important to creating inclusive environments for transgender people. Beginning a conversation by introducing yourself and sharing your pronouns is an easy way to begin a conversation about pronoun usage, and encourages other members of the conversation to follow suit!

'Assuming a stranger's pronouns, or assuming a stranger can know your pronouns based on your appearance contributes to transphobia. No person can "look" like they use a certain pronoun. If a person tells you their pronouns and you are confused about how to use or pronounce them correctly, it is okay to ask for clarification.

'Here are some examples of gender pronouns and how to use them! This is not a complete list of all pronouns that people might use'.

They / Them / Their	They rode their bike to school today by themself. The bike is theirs.
Using the first letter of a person's name as pronouns (Person's name is Taylor)	T rode T's bike to school today by T's self. The bike is T's.
Ze / Hir / Hirs	Ze rode hir bike to school today by hirself. The bike is hirs.
Ey / Em / Eir	Ey rode eir bike to school today by emself. The bike is eirs.
Using a person's name as pronouns (Person's name is Quinn)	Quinn rode Quinn's bike to school today by Quinn's self. The bike is Quinn's.
She / Her / Hers	She rode her bike to school today by herself. The bike is hers.
Ze / Zem / Zir	Ze rode zir bike to school today by zemself. The bike is zirs.
Xe / Xem / Xyr	Xe rode xyr bike to school today by xemself. The bike is xyrs.
He / Him / His	He rode his bike to school today by himself. The bike is his.

To state these variations as fact, to place them into law, to give these tags taxpayers' cash and to re-write male and female sex is wrong. The re-writing of sexuality is harmful and encourages mental health anguish and a very confused generation of young people. It also encourages the campaigners to bully the rest of us into accepting their lifestyle choice whilst the taxpayers fund the industry behind them.

Using the wrong pronouns has crept into our statutes and can get you hefty fines, for example:

In the UK a teacher was suspended after misgendering a transgender pupil by referring to the student as a girl rather than a boy. She was born a boy. The Christian pastor is now suing the school for constructive dismissal and discrimination.

In another UK school a teacher who failed to use the pupil's preferred pronoun, a girl, identifying as a boy, complained to a charity, Mermaid (which receives funding from the taxpayers via the Department for Education). The charity said the child was so distressed by the teacher's words that her mental health suffered and had to take two weeks off school with anxiety and depression.

The girl, her parents and the charity escalated the matter to the Equalities and Human Rights Commission and the police.

New York City's Commission on Human Rights state that employers and landlords who intentionally use the wrong pronouns with their non-binary employees or tenants can face fines of up to $250,000.

Recently, the governor of California (Democratic loon, Jerry Brown) endorsed a bill that threatens to reprimand health professionals who 'wilfully and repeatedly' decline to use a patient's preferred pronouns.

Schools and health departments are following suit by adopting the agenda of 'gender neutrality'. Some have replaced 'biological gender', with the phrase 'sex assigned at birth', meaning that the child will at sometime decide what it's gender shall be.

The lobby will find a cause – build a lobby of activists – give them TV airtime – they get cash from stupid politicians – bullying and confusion reigns.

The UK's most high profile transgender, boxing promoter, Kellie Mahoney, admits to mental illness, suicide and more

Kellie Mahoney, someone I have met, who transitioned from burly boxing promoter and someone who stood for election for Nigel Farage's UKIP, transitioned to a woman.

Kellie said trans people have the highest number of suicide attempt rates.

Speaking about the UK government's latest wheeze to allow people to choose their gender on forms, Kellie said:

Mahoney said the process is "very hard and very intrusive," adding she "attempted suicide a couple of times and one of the most famous times I was found in the street."

However she added that, while she would support the simplification of certain guidelines, "they can't just say you can wake up and [have gender reassignment] I think that's totally wrong.

"If you [could] just wake up and decide and get it done there's no protection and some people could abuse the system".

Kellie is right and open to the abuse of female facilities. Particularly, young girls who should be protected.

One man's view and I suspect he's in the majority …

In this mad cap world of gender, the straight men are sidelined, unless they have sold their soul to gender neutrality. Yet some brave souls are keeping the maleness flag alive.

One summed it up thus, to me:

"Womens Lib means equality and able to smash the glass ceiling…. All wonderful…. but there should always be time for a little chivalry. Which, of course, the feminazis hate and is seen as patronising. The opening of doors, giving up your seat on a train, complimenting dress sense or looks – are all now taboo. It's just courtesy, not sexism.

"I hold the door open for men or women, it's just courtesy. No man has ever given me a disgusted toss of the head and stormed through the door, huffing and puffing about sexism.

"I have seen women ignore pregnant women on trains, expecting the men to give up their seats. I am pleased to do so, but what about a bit of equality here, girls?

"There are benefits to being a woman and as such its only 'natural' that many men wish to embrace their feminine side ..."

He outlines the benefits of transitioning:

Early retirement – become a woman and retire earlier and on the same state pension

Self Preservation – Titanic 'woman and children first', makes sense to be a 'lady' trampling over the real women and children in your size 14 shoes and hairy legs

Opportunities – become a panellist of 'Loose Women' or maybe that's just too frightening

Sport – huge upside, boxing will never be the same ... even Golf, the ladies play on a shorter course and, if you're into track and field, your testosterone will get you a flying start. Or, as we saw recently in the women's US cycling, the man won.

Weary? – people will give up their seat for you on a bus or train

Value – ladies' nights, 2 for 1 drinks and free entry before midnight

Friendship – join the Womens' Institute

Voyeur – Self identify as trans and you'll get to use their bathroom at the gym. Sublime.

And he is not alone. There is a growing backlash against this cultural Marxism. This book is just the beginning.

Chapter 4

The weird world of corporates and our beloved institutions have sadly fallen

Where will it end? Wall Street banks becoming 'right-on' to tech companies being slammed for telling the truth on gender and our high street giants pandering to gender politics.

One well known Wall St bank, eager to divest itself of the evil banker badge and wipe out the banking crisis from their own minds, encourages its employees to watch a video where Steve transes to 'Stacey'. Celebrating diversity, inclusivity and creating a community where colleagues feel comfortable bringing their whole selves into work, they push this narrative for a very small minority.

They then ask employees to embrace Stacey, even encouraging employees to comment and share his/her story. I wonder if there is a thought police section monitoring who clicks through, who doesn't and what goes on their records?

Meanwhile, the traders on the floor look on in embarrassment as Stacey, aka Steve, struts around on high heels, make-up, a dress and a wig, choke on their testosterone while trying to make a buck on the foreign exchange market.

Another friend of mine who works for a large insurance conglomerate told me of a situation where a senior male manager in London for half of the week dresses as a woman, in full make-up, heels, frilly dresses and full hair and the rest of the week dresses as a man, without frills. He says they are made to acknowledge George or Georgina, whichever alter ego whim fits on those days. George/Georgina chooses which toilets to use and even appropriates a different speaking voice, depending on the day. He and his colleagues have no voice on their colleague's voyeurism and nearly everyone finds it off-putting and embarrassing. They do not have the choice to reject his persona and way of life. That is not allowed, it is 'bigoted' and they will be sanctioned. Gay colleagues get angry that they are sidelined but at that same time are included in the LGBTI+ brigade. They do not consider themselves as part of this charade. They are just gay and men, they do not require special treatment, end of story.

I don't know if my US friends have ever seen Little Britain, the TV programme with Matt Lucas and David Walliams where in one sketch they have a man dressed in Victorian ladies clothing. The character keeps insisting she is a woman "I'm a lady", which she keeps having to repeat – because of the beard, body and weird voice, says it all.

To Google. Hero or Devil?

Hailed by its users as a hero, one of the world's best employers to for work, employing thousands around the world, a global giant innovator.

Accused of being the devil incarnate by its enemies for not paying tax to accusations of unfair competition.

The liberal Left's ideal company ... until a gender row blew up in its face.

A man called James Damore has been fired by Google for 'perpetuating gender stereotypes' in a ten page memo to colleagues.

His real crime? Telling the truth, through a politically incorrect memo, that there is a gender difference in attitudes, aptitudes and some are less biologically suited to certain areas of work.

Does common sense, biological fact, years of scientific study into the differences of men and women and real-life observation, show that women operate differently and that men have more interest in tech than women? Despite girls being taught IT at school in equal numbers to boys?

For a company like Google, which promotes a weird, hippy dippy worldview on an all inclusive basis of minority rights, green crap, contempt for conservative values with a liberal Left bias, this truth saying was beyond the pale.

'When it comes to diversity and inclusion,' wrote Damore in his now infamous memo, 'Google's Left-bias has created a politically correct monoculture that maintains its hold by shaming dissenters into silence ...Those with conservative views 'stay in the closet' to avoid hostility".

Yet this is the company that promotes jihadism on YouTube, as the go to site which Google owns, to make your own bombs, how to be a jihadi and blow up the West. It promotes gang culture and killings. So why cannot one of its employees, in an openness that hurts society for the filth they allow on their sites, speak the truth on gender?

Whilst promoting the above, Google lectures us on celebrating diversity, rejecting gender stereotypes and promotes the Anti-Defamation League to block videos that constitute 'hate speech'. One man's hate speech is another man's free speech.

Google has hired a head of diversity, Danielle Brown, who responded with her own memo, saying that Google is "unequivocal in our belief that diversity and inclusion are critical to our success." She said change is hard and "often uncomfortable." Well, it is for those who don't share the liberal Left view of the world.

Let's accept that prejudice did hold women back because of biology and practicalities like having children, etc, and it still does throughout the world through religion and cultures. In the West, the political orthodoxy is that there are now no innate differences between males and females and therefore anybody that suggests otherwise must be the result of social conditioning and prejudice and therefore must be stamped out.

The academic psychologist Lee Jussim, wrote an academic paper entitled "Why brilliant girls tend to favour non-Stem [science, technology, engineering and mathematics] careers". This cited a 2013 survey of more than 1,000 US high school pupils, which found that 70% more girls than boys had strong maths *and* strong verbal skills, while boys were more than twice as likely to have strong maths skills but *not* strong verbal skills.

The authors concluded that their study "provided evidence that it is not lack of ability that causes females to pursue non-Stem careers but rather the greater likelihood that females with high maths ability also have high verbal ability and thus can consider a wider range of occupations than their male peers with high maths ability, who are more likely to have moderate verbal ability".

The latter group — which encompasses the asocial geek on the high-functioning end of the autism spectrum, a condition four times more common among males — finds a welcome in the engineering departments of Silicon Valley.

When you look at Damore and other tech people that you know, what do they have in common? They are geeks, high functioning autistics, socially gauche and mostly male. Girls have had the same opportunities, we just choose different paths as most of us are wired differently to men and that's the unpalatable scientific truth.

Google is also battling with accusation of sexism and discrimination and an investigation on whether it pays women less than men. What utter double standards.

All leading tech companies, such as Google, Facebook and Uber, have all said they are working on improving hiring and working conditions for women. They might be working hard but the numbers have barely changed. Perhaps it's just that women do not want to work for them and that no amount of gender gerrymandering will change that?

And there is a higher propensity of people in the autistic spectrum working in IT. Autism is mainly attributed to males.

And when a sensible corporate tries to stop fraud at a bank ...

A transitioning person was prevented from accessing his/her bank account because a call centre operative did not recognise the voice on the phone as transitioning person, and treated the woman as a man.

Of course they would. If we want to stop bank fraud, checks are put in place for exactly this reason.

The woman complained that she was asked to take her passport into the bank branch to prove who she was. Unfortunately, her passport was being processed to reflect her new identity.

Well, she can't have it both ways, although she wishes to sexually.

You can't win if you are on the other side of sensible and the bank concerned should not be twisting and turning in agony over any offence caused. This person is in a tiny minority.

Gender neutralizing our children's clothes

Big business is poking its nose into gender, as we have seen with Facebook and Twitter. We have high street brands deciding on environmentalism and now sexuality and how we shop for children's clothes.

The UK's top middle class store of choice, John Lewis (shrine for food, drink, cosmetics, clothes and furniture), announced last year they were gender neutralising children's clothes. No longer would they label knickers, anything pink or frilly, bras or tights as 'girls' items', nor would they label anything blue, underpants (with slits for willies), formal suits and shirts as 'boys' items' to 'avoid reinforcing gender stereotypes'.

I visited the store the day after this announcement – the day before kids go back to school – only to find that the boys shoes were in the boys section and, you've guessed it, the girls were in the girls section, along with school uniforms separated and, thankfully, they had left the baby section alone (although that changed later).

So does 10-year-old little Johnny need a grey school jumper sized Medium or Aged 10 or size 8? Is a traditional boys age 10 shirt the same size as a traditional girls age 10? Are the buttons on the same side? Is a boy's blazer cut the same way as a girls blazer?

I recently visited the babies department a couple of months ago. It's a mess unless you are buying new born, which seems mainly to be items of clothing in cream or white. Safe.

Go above 3 months and you'll find little trousers and waistcoat sets in beige and blue. Boys you would think? Not so, it's jumbled up between girly pink and frilly dresses. Good luck in finding a suitable outfit. The whole layout is a mess.

Ignoring the arguments about whether boys can wear pink or girls can wear camouflage ... simple logistics means boys and girls are generally different sizes at the same age. These gender liberals may think that Darwin was an Imperialistic

Slave Denying Naturalist Fascist, but like it or not the anatomy of the sexes is different.

John Lewis has built a brand on traditional values of quality and service but it is now just giving in to appease a minority of so called-liberals, for whom whatever you do will never be enough anyway. Why stop at children's clothing? How dare they have sections called Menswear and Ladieswear? If my husband wanted to buy a little off the shoulder sparkly top then he should be allowed to - next the to Y-fronts - rather than be forced to embarrass himself by shopping in the ladies section?

They are not alone. As the feminizis mount campaigns for gender neutral toys, the labels are taken down instore, as in the case of Marks and Spencer.

As retail outlets try to deconstruct sex as something to be ignored, disregarded, and renamed as 'labelling' cosmetics sales are going through the roof, teenagers are obsessed with how they look, Instagram is booming, selfies abound, Sugar Daddy websites are doing a sterling trade, women line up to stalk and bed pop stars, filmstars and soccer players - so they can reflect in their men's glories, their wealth, the magazine deals, to work as a WAG (wives and girlfriends), but not an engineer, how the feminiazis rail against them. These women have had more equal sex education aimed at them like no other generation yet, they want to be kept women. They will shove the existing WAG off her perch, over a cliff, to take her place. Non-existent is the sisterhood for the wannabe WAG. She wants to own the latest Gucci bag, Jimmy Choos, hair extensions and will get herself pregnant to be kept on the payroll, even when she's pushed off her perch, it keeps the tabloids interested, particularly if she names the poor child some ridiculous name, like Pixie Fifi Trixiebell. These women will forever carry the Barbie torch, long after the current wave of feminazis are well into their pension years.

Despite the feminazis campaign for sexless clothes, education, work, human nature will prevail, you can't remove genes, sex - what attracts people: sex and good looks. Sex attracts which makes babies and keeps the human race alive. You might just as well wipe humans out and let robots take over.

In a world where Starbucks avoids tax but preaches on gay marriage, having a louder voice than the leader of the Church of England, is it any wonder that big business is moving into a new morality based on sexuality and shopping?

Shoe retailer gets in hot water over 'Dolly Babe' and 'Leader' terms for shoes

When I was growing up I was dragged by my mother to a shop called 'Clarks' because they measured your feet accurately using a type of x-ray machine (now banned). It was fascinating to see this very clever machine encircle my feet and suggest a size. My only problem was that my mother did not have the same idea of style and fashion as I did.

Clarks came under fire recently because they became embroiled in a sexist shoe row for naming a new girls range as 'Dolly Babe' and the boys as 'Leader'. Yep, you can see where this is leading …

And now they have gone all gender neutral. They recently announced they now have a gender neutral ethos ….' So, from 2018 onwards they will have more unisex shoes. They have caved in to the pressure for giving their shoes ridiculous names.

Didn't anyone in the PR department think that there would be a backlash for 'Dolly Babes', it sounds more like a porn site than a name for children's shoes.

We now have a global company who, before this silly row, was doing what they do best, selling robust and easy to wear shoes. Now they have an 'ethos of gender neutrality'.

The beauty industry – when lipsticks are politicised

Trans person sacked from L'Oreal UK, because it's worth it

A transgender person was sacked by L'Oreal UK for posting that all white people are guilty of racism and we benefit through white privilege.

It's good to see that a cosmetics company is standing up to reverse racism. But are we not worried that free speech is being stamped out? As a black, middle class, privileged, trans model, she is preaching bullshit, but shouldn't we defend her right of free speech?

This person is a bit silly because where else would she get the chance to earn considerable amounts of money as a model? That was not enough for this person, the mere fact that being employed as a trans and black, she had made the grade. Shouting off about white privilege and racism has no place nor influence on whether we decide to buy a red or pink lipstick, whether you are black, white or brown.

I hope this competitive victimhood identity politics world will have its day soon and we will look back and think, it was just a phase they were going through.

There is no justification for this costly nonsense. In 2015 the Office for National Statistics stated that 1.7% of the UK population identified themselves as lesbian, gay or bisexual (LGB). This small majority and their vociferous campaigners are driving an agenda that does not reflect society and just alienates the rest of us. I make a point of not buying goods or services from these companies that are bowing to left wing group think. If they were not so overt about their storylines and included all sections of society, rather than the concentration that is currently on our screens, no one would bat an eyelid.

The advertising industry in the UK is getting in on the right-on act. Shunning the majority of white, heterosexual Britain, for fear of being called bigots. Recent advertisemetns on TV have seen same sex couples buying houses; women kissing in a banking advert; and Tiffany's the jeweller, ran a gay marriage proposal ad. A third of advertisers said they had used fewer heterosexual couples over the past year.

Not to be left out, our multi billion tech industry has gone all cuddly and gender neutral.

Take Facebook.

In 2014 you could self-identify on Facebook with a choice (non-binary choice, I suppose) of 58 varieties of gender .... and rising.

In 2015, after being told by users that its 58 existing gender options are not inclusive enough, the social network has relented and given its US-based members a chance to fill in their own gender as they wish:

"Now, if you do not identify with the pre-populated list of gender identities, you are able to add your own. As before, you can add up to 10 gender terms and also have the ability to control the audience with whom you would like to share your custom gender. We recognize that some people face challenges sharing their true gender identity with others, and this setting gives people the ability to express themselves in an authentic way," Facebook's Diversity team said in a statement.

"We're hoping this will open up the dialogue," said Ari Chivukula, a transgender member of the team.

Not to be left out: Twitter

Thankfully, Twitter is playing along too. They have a special area for Lesbians Who Tech. They twitter on … *"We are also focused on sexual orientation and gender identity. In 2016 for the first time, we gave all US new hires the opportunity to self-identify as LGBTQ. While this data collection is new and therefore limited, we wanted those who chose to identify to be counted. Of employees answering, 10% identified as LGBTQ. As more employees respond in 2017, we expect to have a more complete picture."* Jeffrey Siminoff, VP, Inclusion & Diversity, Twitter

Our national and treasured institutions

The National Trust - charitable keeper of the UK's national treasurers and now ... gender too

If you visit the UK you and want to see many of our grand houses, castles and heritage sites you can, thanks to the kind generosity of the public who pay to belong to the charity, the National Trust.

Generous people have bequeathed their house for many reasons - some because of the evil death tax, others for altruistic reasons and some because they have too many houses.

Whatever reason, they did not do so for the National Trust to start bullying their employees and their army of volunteers to celebrity diversity and gender politics.

Many are not employees but volunteers, without whom the National Trust could not operate, dedicate their time for the love of our heritage.

Many of the fee paying members are families and elderly people, most are not into virtue signalling and certainly not social justice warriors.

Yet the National Trust felt it had to bully its employees and volunteers to virtue signal their support of diversity by wearing rainbow decorated lanyards.

Those who refused to do so were asked 'not to be on duty in a visitor facing role'. The NT felt by wearing a lanyard we are sending a clear message of welcome to all of our visitors'. This is pure, unadulterated diversity bullying bullshit.

I tweeted to them: why are you bullying your volunteers to self-identify, most of them would say Mrs or Mr? Their reply was, " …this is not compulsory, but voluntary". I am sure the retired bank manager in charge of Azaleas at a stately home is being watched for his subversiveness.

Volunteers felt they were being judged as transphobic and intolerant for refusing to wear a rainbow coloured lanyard. They wanted to keep their views on the LGBTQ+ industry private, if they ever gave it a thought at all.

Speaking on the ever right, Breitbart London, Benjamin Harris-Quinney, chairman of The Bow Group, Britain's oldest conservative think tank, told Breitbart London: *"I think the vast majority of people in Britain believe that someone's sexual preference is a private matter for them.*

"However, what we are seeing is a movement not in the interests of that commitment to personal choice and freedom, but to the exact opposite: tyranny.

"That we have reached a point as a nation where the question is genuinely being asked 'Should it be compulsory to wear an LGBT Pride badge?' is a chilling indictment of a movement which is about political extremism, not freedom."

Well, here we are folks. What was once parody is now reality in Britain.

Mr. Harris-Quinney added: *"The foundation of this movement is Cultural Marxism, the hard left wing desire to use identity politics to erode and destroy the cultural pillars of the Judeo-Christian West.*

"The speed as a society which we have gone from changing our laws in the supposed interests of 'equality' to forcing people to accept a political ideology will alarm most British people who are firmly against the forced acceptance of any political views.

"It is becoming clear what opponents of this movement have said all along: People who are part of the LGBT lobby are not acting in the interests of gay people but a far darker totalitarian and extremist cause that is rightly opposed by the vast majority of our citizens."

I cancelled our National Trust membership.

Girl Guides

When in 1909, a group of girls appeared at a Boy Scout Rally in the UK declaring themselves to the Girl Scouts, Lord Baden-Powell, the founder of the Boy Scouts, decided that there should be a movement for girls. Guiding was introduced that year and responded to the specific needs of girls and young women.

Remember that phrase, 'responded to the specific needs of girls and young women'.

Now renamed as 'Girl Guiding', it recently hit the headlines for introducing a policy of allowing trans people to work with their Girl Guides and allowing trans-girls (boys) to join.

When a group of parents wrote a letter to a newspaper expressing their concern, along with two Guide leaders, they were expelled.

Girl Guiding is about 'girls', the boys have their own Scouting arrangement and also allow girls.

However, the Guides got into trouble because they still ban trans boys (actual girls) from joining. They expect girls to share showers and tents with boys.

I have repeatedly asked the Girl Guides what safety guidelines have they put in place to protect the actual girls? My letter in full:

Amanda Medler, Chief Guide
and
Ruth Marvel, Acting Chief Executive
Girlguiding UK

Dear Ms Medler and Ms Marvel

Following the recent media interest on your treatment of 'trans' issues and the sacking of staff members, your subsequent statements and your Diversity policy on your website, I would like to ask the following questions, firstly as a mother and secondly as a politician:

1. You state that 86% of those surveyed through the Girls' Attitudes Survey said that they did not think people should be discriminated against because they are transgender. Could you please tell me how many people received this survey?
2. How many parents have objected to your trans policies?
3. How many parents have withdrawn their daughters from your organisation because of your trans policies?

4. How many trans boys a) have applied in the last two years and b) how many trans boys are currently active in troupes?
5. In your diversity policy statement you state that you take into consideration the boys' who are 'trans' at all times. You refer to **their** needs through the statements ensuring that **their** needs to share bathrooms and accommodation with normal girls, who are your majority, are taken into account. Could you tell me what you do if normal girls object to sharing bathroom facilities and accommodation with the trans boys?
6. Why is the emphasis on trans boys rather than the majority of girls in your care?
7. What safeguarding policies do you have in place to protect ordinary girls and young women from sexual advances from trans boys – both trans girl guiding boys and the leadership who are male but identifying as a woman?
8. You have a page dedicated to Muslim Girl Guiding. Could you tell me what policy advice you give to Muslim girls and their parents who are expected to accommodate trans boys in their troupe, in shared accommodation and shared bathroom facilities?
9. Have any Muslim parents objected, have girls been withdrawn or do you operate separate troupes for Muslim girls?

As leading charities operating in the 'trans' sphere state, and our own NHS too, that body dysphoria only makes up 1% of the population (and the same is true in all advanced Western democracies), you feel that you are under pressure to provide for trans boys rather than the majority of normal girls?

It was sent in October, I have yet to receive a reply.

Chapter 5

Transgender and children

The first rule of government is to keep us safe.

I think one of the worst aspects of the transgender agenda is the corruption and defilement of our little children.

Who knew that children as young as three were being treated for gender dysphoria?

Yes, you read right - for *children*. Build a campaign, an industry smells cash and publicity, politicians give them the cash and they target our children.

The market for child transgenderism has quadrupled in five years.

Just a short few years ago we were debating whether schools should be teaching 'age appropriate' sexuality to our children. And at what age should we discuss how babies are made? We have now made this huge leap to discussing LGBT 'rights' to five year olds. Who asked the parents? Who voted for this?

Teachers are being forced to impart gender issues which is the feminazi indoctrination of our children with political goals and tick box teaching, more concerned with encouraging children to think about gender and sexuality in new ways, than teaching our children STEM subjects and allowing them to play and be brought up unhindered by this dangerous thinking. The role of the teacher becomes policing the values, thoughts and language of children to bring them in line with one particular ideological position. Their childhoods are then mired in confusion and the questionning of their sexuality, instead of protecting our kids, they're indoctrinating and ending their childhood.

The industry even has its own clinic, funded by our NHS, the Gender Identity Development Service (GIDS). The clinic saw 2000 children in 2017, 84 of the little mites were only aged between 3 and 7 years old. This is compared to 20 in 2012/13.

In 2016 there were a total of 2,106 referrals for children aged between three and 18 years, more than six times the 314 referrals in the previous five years.

A British newspaper, the Mail on Sunday, recently revealed the shocking numbers of English (there are separate figures for Wales, Scotland and Northern Ireland) children who are being subjected to horrific sex changing medication.

In the UK more than 800 children in England, some as young as ten, are being fed drugs to help them change gender, paid for by the taxpayer and available on our cash strapped National Health Service. Of the 800, 230 of them are under the age of 14.

It is available to those who 'believe' they are trapped in the wrong body. Powerful monthly hormone injections stop the development of sex organs, breasts and body hair, making it easier for Frankenstein doctors to carry out sex swap surgery later.

How do they know they are 'trapped' in the wrong body? Answer: because of the pernicious and well-funded evil lobby that prey on their young minds and vulnerability.

Earlier this year three top US doctors, Professors Paul Hurz, Paul McHugh and Lawrence Mayer, published a highly critical report on the use of puberty-blockers to treat gender dysphoria.

Writing in American academic journal The New Atlantis, they warned that the safety of this 'experimental' treatment was 'unsupported by rigorous scientific evidence'.

They further argued that the use of such drugs may be driving children to 'persist in identifying as transgender'

Yet, the Frankenstein brigade carry on regardless.

One son of Frankenstein said, "We're lucky in the UK that people don't miss out - they will get this treatment." It's like they're selling a new powerful brand of soap powder.

Another Frankenstein at a London clinic, funded by British cash-strapped National Health Service, says "There has been significant progress towards the acceptance and recognition of transgender and gender-diverse people in our society. There is also greater knowledge about specialist gender clinics and the pathways into them, and an increased awareness of the possibilities around treatments."

Yes, reality TV stars changing their sex, what makes for fun TV that says more about their bank accounts and notoriety than gender dysphoria, has a profound effect on young minds. The 'pathways' are state funded clinics and charities compounding the wealth of information out there, together with government collusion. All young minds and gullible parents need is an internet connection.

Having raised two boys and two step-children, all now in their twenties, kids are not old enough to make those decisions. We are all confused at puberty. Our bodies change, the hormones kick in, we are tearful, angry, horrid and ashamed of our changing bodies, hair and voices.

From an early age I climbed trees, fought to be Batman (I was never Cat Woman!), built go-karts and preferred boys company to girls. That didn't make me or anyone else transgender, just a tomboy. And sometimes I played with my Barbie or at being 'house'. I also fired cap guns and played at cowboys and Indians (or should that now be cowpersons and people of indigenous roots?).

Girls are notoriously good at having crushes on teachers, fellow pupils and will feel closer to their girlfriends than boys or their parents. This does not make them self identify as trans, nor lesbian, but is a perfectly normal function of growing up, puberty and hormones. With the wealth of funded material now found on the internet, I am hardly surprised they are confused.

If you look for problems, you can always find them.

Kids and their parents are being indulged by an experimental nightmare that is unethical and costly in terms of cash and lives.

As explained before, if there's a gap in the market for a cause and a pot of money attached, they will come.

Gender Neutral Nonsense - raising kids

In few years ago two Nordic parents decided to raise their child as gender neutral. No one knew the sex of the child, except for those who changed its nappy.

These mentally ill parents, or child abusers, if you want to be really hard on them, say their decision was rooted in the feminist philosophy that gender is a social construction.

"We want X to grow up more freely and avoid being forced into a specific gender mould from the outset," X's mother said. "It's cruel to bring a child into the world with a blue or pink stamp on their forehead."

The child's parents said so long as they keep X's gender a secret, he or she will be able to avoid preconceived notions of how people should be treated if male or female.

X's wardrobe includes everything from dresses to trousers and X's hairstyle changes on a regular basis. And X usually decides how X is going to dress on a given morning.

Although X knows that there are physical differences between a boy and a girl, X's parents never use personal pronouns when referring to the child – they just say X.

"I believe that the self-confidence and personality that X has shaped will remain for a lifetime," said X's mother. Although we are not sure whether X's mother is really the mother, or the father, or gender neutral.

It will be interesting to psychoanalyse X in a few years time or follow X's progress through school life. Will X have friends, will X be accepted by other parents and invited to birthday parties and will X be happy?

In Sweden, the gender brainwashing has risen to epic levels. Sweden has gone to extraordinary lengths to impose gender neutrality in classrooms, regularly filming teachers' interactions with children and analysing them for gender bias.

Sweden's teachers should be teaching, not policing.

In Canada and a few other countries this dangerous experiment is slowly increasing.

We do not know the long terms effects of these 'progressive' topsy turvy experiments. The kids we do know about are now living in remote communities, presumably to continue their experiment or is it because they do not want their weird lifestyles and child abuse exposed and condemned? Most are home schooled. That tells you more about the parents than the poor kids at this stage.

I have read so many stories of people 'coming out' in liberal Left newspapers, never queried for their weirdness or acceptability:

A boy: 'I learned what it was to be trans through YouTube … I didn't know what it was, I was just trying to Google myself. Until I was four or five I didn't know I was a girl … I was yelled at by a teacher when I was six years old because I went to the toilet with the girls." Where were his parents while this poor child was confused? He didn't know what sex he was? Come on.

Another, a boy (I think): "Most people you read about are usually one type of trans person … they're usually binary (identify as either male or female), they usually pass as someone as that gender, they're usually white and always known that they're identified as the 'wrong gender'. I'm non-binary – I don't always identify as male or female. There are lots of sub-section – gender fluid, bi-gender, a demi-girl or a demi-boy. I identify as non-binary and don't put myself into a sub-category. Some days a like to be a woman, other days I'm a man … I'm pretty much anything at the moment. I don't want to be part of any mainstream movement …".

When researching this book I wondered when 'white privilege' would rear its head. Thinking about it, perhaps there is a white privilege element to this gender indulgement, have we become so rich, so cossetted and so inward looking, we as humans like to find or create struggle? Is gender the next struggle? If so, it's a pretty poor one, Youtube, Google and the clinics have a lot to answer for as I certainly do not understand these confused persons' problems. The problems are invented, not real.

Transgender and the bathroom issue

Most of us would like this to be water under the bridge or loo.

Why is it acceptable that the opposite sex can use the bathroom of the other sex? Going to the bathroom has always been a pretty private necessity.

In the UK, our schools are under financial and political pressure. We have an eye-watering national debt because of proligate governments, including conservative ones. Cutbacks have been made in our schools and our teachers tell us they are underfunded, overworked and underpaid. We want our children to succeed and their teachers too but increasingly money is being wasted on unnecessary sexual agendas.

A leading UK academic, Dr Joanna Williams, has claimed that introducing transgender policies in schools is a waste of time and taxpayers' money, and only confuses children further. Hear hear.

She goes on to say, "We are increasingly reminded that schools are struggling financially. Yet the time, effort and money that goes into producing and monitoring Transgender Policies is out of all proportion to the tiny number of trans children currently in British schools.

"By the time they start school, most children know their name, how old they are and where they live.

"Most also know for certain whether they are a boy or a girl. Despite this, many primary schools now have policies in place 'to support trans children' and to 'provide a broad overview of the needs of transgender children and their families'."

She notes that "However politically well intentioned teachers may be, criticising the views and values of home vastly alters the remit of the school away from education and towards the promotion of a distinct political outlook."

She's right. Schools are learning environments. Yes, they also provide support services but wasting scarce cash on gender neutral bathrooms is politically correct madness. We should be spending time and cash on STEM subjects as we need more engineers, mathematicians, scientists and medics, to compete in a global world.

In the US, Obama was at the heart of this damaging piece of legislation:

"Schools have a responsibility to provide a safe and non-discriminatory environment for all students, including transgender students," the guidance read, in part. "A school may not require transgender students to use facilities inconsistent with their gender identity or to use individual-user facilities when other students are not required to do so."

Thankfully, under President Trump, companies and family groups are fighting back.

In Austin, Texas, more than 50 Houston business leaders, including the heads of some of the US's top oil companies, are opposing a Texas "bathroom bill" targeting transgender people - adding to an already long list of powerful firms opposing it.

In a letter to Gov. Greg Abbott, the business leaders wrote that they support "diversity and inclusion" and that "any such bill risks harming Texas' reputation and impacting the state's economic growth." Its signers included executives from Chevron, Shell, ConocoPhillips and ExxonMobil.

Gov Abbott is leading the way and has called state lawmakers into a special legislative session after a bill requiring transgender Texans to use public restrooms corresponding to the gender on their birth certificates which failed in May 2017

In Montana, a conservative group, The Montana Family Foundation launched its campaign to place the matter on the 2018 fall ballot after lawmakers declined to do so.

If approved by voters, the measure would affect how public schools, universities and other government agencies accommodate transgender people.

The foundation called the effort a necessary step to protect "the privacy, safety and dignity" of Montana children and help guard against sexual predators.

"There are active lawsuits in other states, and we wanted to take a proactive role in protecting privacy," said Bowen Greenwood, director of government affairs for the foundation.

In Britain, it was ten years ago since the barmy burghers of Manchester University introduced gender free toilets. And then other left wing councils followed, bowing to the left wing militants, ignoring the majority.

Their 'reasonable' counterargument is that all domestic homes share bathrooms. Yes, but sharing a bathroom with your wife and kids is a bit different to sharing a bathroom with men who define as women.

Any woman that has had to queue for the loo at a theatre or concert does not want to share with a man wearing a dress.

This 'trans tyranny' of the bathroom is not about trans rights or the right on virtue signallers, it's about forcing the rest of us to accept the completely unacceptable behaviour of the left for a very small minority of people.

There is a campaign in the UK to de-sex every public toilet and even primary schools to accommodate the 'needs' of a very small number of people.

Unfortunately, the voices of those who worry about their children being groomed by paedophiles cross dressing and identifying as trans who may lurk in our toilets are waived away as hate crime.

Or the burly football player who, after ten cans of beer, decides that it would be fun to pee in the women's loos, pretending he's trans.

Or when you take your daughter to the loo when she is going through puberty and using sanitary towels because of her period. Do you think she really wants to use the sanitary dispenser in front of a trans man?

When we're washing our hands at the sink do we really want a trans person watching us adjusting our stockings and skirts? Or, asking your friend, "Does my bum look big in this?".

It's an age thing too. I can remember visiting the ladies' loo at Buckingham Palace when I was a guest at the Queen's summer garden party. There was a butch lesbian dressed in a suit, tie, shaved head and brogues. I watched the various older women present gasp and do a double take at the person queuing, some were uncomfortable. I could see she was a lesbian but some of the refined ladies of rural England did not. I wonder if the men would have liked her in the men's loo while they were using the urinal?

I think this young lady speaks for most of us:

"It just doesn't feel right knowing someone with male anatomy is in the bathroom with me. I have nothing against Student A and would be her friend if I knew her better, but when it comes down to it, I don't feel right changing in the same room as a transgender student. The locker room is already filled with so much judgment, and I barely feel OK changing in front of my naturally born girl peers."

Taking it to the limit - Drag Queen Story Time for schools (one import from the US you can keep)

In San Francisco, Drag Queens are delivering story time in schools and its being offered to us Brits.

I love a drag queen. I've been to London's Madam Jo Jo's club a few times, where men dress as women in wonderful dresses, wigs, too much make-up, high heels to die for … and they do a brilliant rendition of Abba songs and Starship

Trooper. There is an annual drag queen race in Greenwich to raise money for HIV which we attend. I watch them hobble about on their oversize platform shoes in Soho on a Saturday morning whilst enjoying lunch at an upstairs restaurant, sans make-up and clad in leopard print clothes, as they shop for fruit and veg. They pass the local mosque, mostly closed, I wonder what our resident tolerants think of them?

But do I think 'Drag Queen Story Time' delivered by old and young drag queens is a good idea in our schools? No, but it is coming to a school near you soon to 'challenge intolerance and homophobia at a young age'. Oh, and they do racism too. I do object to racism and disability being lumped into transgender nonsense, they're totally different issues.

Based on an American project (thanks, not), they are currently Crowdfunding to raise money to roll it out across Bristol, a British City.

We are admonished by the language we use. Take 'trannies', a term most trannies use to describe themselves, but the thought police say this is wrong. My friend, Tranny, from Soho, describes and signs his emails and texts as Tranny. He hates the political correctness and objects to others being offended on his behalf and what he calls himself. (See ch 11, Trannie).

Transgender children are being indulged and abused

It seems the British government's NHS recognises and produces materials for children from the age of 15 years, publishing a number of information booklets and further advice.

http://www.mermaidsuk.org.uk/assets/media/17-15-02-A-Guide-For-Young-People.pdf (More about Mermaids, later)

Why then are publicly funded bodies encouraging gender altering at such an early and tender age?

The British Broadcasting Company (BBC) is a taxpayer funded media outlet. Their children's flagship programme for 6-12 year olds is CBBC.

In 2014 they made a series called 'My Life', one such programme was about Leo:
"Leo is 13. He loves hanging around with his friends, beat-boxing, playing football and doing all the things you'd expect a 13-year-old boy to do. But Leo was born a girl. He was named Lily by his mum and dad, who thought they had another daughter. However, from an early age, Leo knew he wasn't a girl. He is a boy but born in a girl's body. In this intimate documentary, Leo tells his story. He shares poignant moments from his video diary with CBBC viewers to detail his journey to get his first male passport and be accepted as a boy". First shown on CBBC 17th Nov 2014 (UK)
https://www.youtube.com/watch?v=0x_u2cs8DpI

At 11 years Lilly had her name changed to Leo. Her mother realised her daughter really wanted to be a boy when Lilly shouted at her one day, "I want to be a boy!".

Following this over-indulged child he was feted in the media, fawned over by morning TV sofa journalists and was rather surprised when savaged in the right leaning press. The programme unsurprisingly won a BAFTA.

He was invited to the House of Commons in London. He said didn't know what Big Ben was and had never travelled outside of the UK. How on earth could a child with so little education and knowledge know she was a boy? It's the internet and the well-funded campaign groups. Could you imagine what this child with such an active imagination could achieve if channelled in the right direction?

People were rightly outraged that this type of programme was aired to young, impressionable children.

Attacking their critics, one campaigner said, 'I wonder how many people have had training in trans issues?'. And there you have it, the rest of us have to be 'trained' and then we will accept.

Moving on to the US.

The current 'trend' and fad for trans is mostly conducted in California.

They are asking why the sudden surge of transgender teens?

A transgender therapist notes, 'Transgenderism has become a specialty for me. I've seen much more growth in the last two years – even more than last year.' Build it, promote it, stick it up on a website, YouTube it, give it public funding and they will come.

One girl, 12, described how she liked playing with action figures and liked sports. She said she didn't feel like a boy or a girl. When she found out about 'agender' she almost cried. Yes, it's called the world wide web and all sorts get posted, and some are even funded. This girl should have carried on playing with her action figures and excelling in sports, rather than poking around on the internet.

And the parents are no better. A number of parents have described how instead of discouraging their teenage children to trans or seek counselling for them, they call or them, they call a helpline and asked to join to get themselves 'educated'. The right-on nutters of California.

One 14-years-old boy started identifying as a girl but wouldn't wear girls clothes, hang out with girls and doesn't even shave his moustache, attended a trans clinic, they recommended hormone replacement therapy.

The parents, self-describe as ultra-liberals, Hillary loving, vegetarian west coasters, wouldn't let their child go down that route, "Well, we don't even let her eat chicken with hormones or bleach".

Too many parents are living their lives through their children. When your teenage Tom announces he's becoming Tina, the mother (usually) embraces him, buys him a whole new wardrobe and finds him a quack that will prescribe hormone blockers.

In a random sample of 6-8th graders in San Francisco, children were asked if they identified as male, female or transgendered – 1.3% ticked the trans box.

Where is this all coming from? Experts say it is the internet – YouTube binges and social contagion, others blame daytime TV, and trans activists masquerading as therapists and parents. Parents who embrace and indulge the child's tendencies and exploration are seen as socially rewarded, accepting and enlightened. Some see it as a way to have reflected glory in getting their kids a modelling or TV contract. While those who try traditional parenting are seen as unaccepting, lacking in compassion, empathy and … even worse, conservative.

Parents are becoming lazy in many ways, both in the US and UK, where it is all too difficult to be a parent. Busy jobs, lives, social media, wanting to be the children's friend rather than a parent, instead of enforcing rules and boundaries, love, vigilance and patience. We have allowed this craze to fester and it's about time we took back control of our kids, instead of Google dictating our lives. Fashions come and go and I hope this is one fashion item that is discarded pretty soon.

Instead of taking a rational approach and treating it as a psychosocial issue we are sleep-walking into a radical ideological experiment.

One sane parent describes this current trend as a 'fad' and I think she's right. She describes the hyper sexuality of girls and the pressures on them to be ultra thin, to have long, shiny hair, flawless skin, large breasts and to post as many beautiful pictures as possible on social media. It's tiring, un-natural and unrealistic and puts enormous pressures on girls. Not fitting in with the in-crowd is terribly crushing for girls and I think a lot of the asexual behaviour – and it is not all trans nonsense, is a backlash and protest against the sexualisation of our teenage girls.

I sometimes wonder if parents lead such boring lives that they use their children to upscale their fun?

ElleUS magazine promotes a mother and her 8-year-old son as drag queen 'Lactatia'. Is it simply a mother's right to do this?

You judge.
https://t.co/eK7iZXUeo3

The sexualisation of our children isn't just confined to the liberal Left.

Muslims in the UK are forcing headscarves on young children, some as young as five, thereby sexualising them:

In the politically correct world of our London Muslim Mayor, he has, thankfully, abandoned an advertising campaign seemingly sexualising young children, sanctioned by Boris Johnson (Conservative, former Mayor, former Foreign Secretary and now leading Brexiteer, albeit on the back benches). British transport chiefs have been forced to drop a children's road safety campaign depicting a Muslim nursery schoolgirl wearing a religious headscarf.

The £2 million campaign was accused of sexualising a child because the hijab is traditionally worn by women only from puberty as a sign of female modesty in front of men. The images are included in children's books distributed through nurseries and in stories on a website.

The Children's Traffic Club London, promoted by Transport for London (TfL), has recruited more than 66,000 children across the capital.

TfL, which is chaired by Sadiq Khan, the capital's Labour mayor, apologised and said that it would stop using the images.

The books were introduced under his Conservative predecessor Boris Johnson in 2015.

The stories are illustrated with characters from ethnically diverse backgrounds. The Muslim girl, aged three or four, is called Razmi and is always shown wearing a religious headscarf. Razmi is seen indoors in the home of a Chinese girl and that child's grandmother and on outings.

Gina Khan, an advocate of Islamic women's equality, said: "You are sexualising a four-year-old girl. It is as simple as that. The reason a female is covered is so men don't look at her. How can you integrate in society if you have a four-year-old girl wearing a hijab?"

Shaista Gohir, chairwoman of the Muslim Women's Network UK charity, said: "It's like trying to get that child to try to grow up far too quickly. A child needs to be treated like a child."

She criticised the tendency of the media to stereotype by always portraying Muslim women as wearing headscarves when many choose not to. Such a depiction in an educational book sent a message to boys that girls are supposed to cover their hair, she suggested.

The books produced by the Children's Traffic Club London, promoted by Transport for London, were distributed through nurseries and in stories on a website.

Aisha Ali-Khan, a Muslim feminist campaigner, said the publishers of the book need diversity training. "The hijab is a Saudi-isation of British Muslim identity," she said. "If you are a Muslim girl and look at these images and see this girl is Muslim and she is wearing a hijab and you aren't, you will think there's something wrong with you. It is far too young. You are a child. What are you being modest for?"

I disagree with Ali-Khan, the authors do not need 'diversity training', they should just be aware of cultural norms.

Dame Louise Casey, the government's integration tsar, intervened in a row in Birmingham this year when a Catholic school came under pressure to let a four-year-old girl wear a Muslim headscarf. She has expressed concern that "time and again I found it was women and children who were the targets of these [kind of] regressive practices" against the vulnerable.

The London road safety books take pains to emphasise diversity. An Irish-origin child is taken, wearing a shamrock-emblazoned hat, to celebrate St Patrick's Day in Trafalgar Square with "hundreds of happy people all dressed in green". A middle-class white boy is taken by his father to watch the tennis at Wimbledon while a black man takes his niece to play football in the park.

A TfL spokeswoman said: "We apologise for any offence caused by this content and we will not use these designs in future."

This madness is sexualising young children as headscarves are generally not worn by Muslim girls until puberty.

Muslims and the politically correct appeasers suggests that they are 'just trying to be like mum'. But what if other daughters just wanted to be like 'mum' and wore lipstick, short skirts and push up bras to school?

I mention this story because it is sexualising and interfering with our children's right to be loved, sheltered and treated like children, rather than pandering to a minority and a religion that does not respect women's rights.

In the UK, Muslim girls as young as five are increasingly made to wear veils by their parents, sanctioned by schools, as part of school uniform policies. (see earlier chapter).

This is detrimental to women's historical fight for equality in our secular democracy. It is bowing to a politicised and radical Islamic agenda.

This is about the power of men over women, control, status and backward honour codes. It is political correctness gone mad in the name of 'religious freedom', and is totally against our liberal and secular society – and women.

It is more sexualisation of our children, but this time in the name of religious extremism and has no place in our schools.

State funded BBC TV for children

Who authorised the BBC to start brainwashing our children into believing that multiculturalism, LBG and trans was normal?

For decades the BBC was a brilliant channel for children. It was safe to Watch with Mother, or not. Parents didn't have to worry about the content, they could plonk them down in front of the TV and cook the dinner. Children's TV was created for the innocent, untainted minds. No more.

The state-funded BBC now that they have no real identity. From programmes for transitioning 8-year-olds; making programmes about converting to Islam while not requiring Islamic schools to teach about the tolerance of Christianity; encouraging children to fast/ban pork from menus; Thomas the Tank Engine is now re-written, the past erased to show multicultural Britain with gender equality (I don't know how they're going to deal with the shaming fat issues of the 'Fat Controller'); Sesame Street's Bert and Ernie are now a gay couple; they re-write history with programmes depicting ethnic, women and LGBT characters in roles playing the parts that were factually and historically male.

The majority of parents want to keep their children safe, safe from indoctrination, safe from confusing gender nonsense, safe until their little minds can understand some minorities are different but not the norm.

There is something nasty and rotten at the core from the people that are pushing this agenda to tots.

BBC using children as social experiments

The BBC is having a hard time in the UK at the moment for its innate liberal left group think on most subjects from Brexit, to gender, to economics and for being anti conservative.

They are also dipping their toes into social experimentation which seems to have backfired.

The BBC describe the show as a "bold, engaging and provocative experiment" which is the inspiration of medical doctor Javid Abdelmoneim.

According to the BBC, the doctor "aims to remove all differences in the way boys and girls are treated to see if, after six weeks of "gender neutral" treatment, he can even out the gaps in their achievement across a range of important psychological measures from self-confidence to spatial awareness".

Dr Abdelmoneim said: "Girls significantly underestimate how clever they are and have less self esteem. Boys can't express their emotions except for anger, which is really disturbing."

The doctor introduces a series of "interventions" to "gender neutralise" the class of 23 children, but by the end of the programme he has misgivings.

"I'm worried that all I've done is upset a load of kids and none of this has had the slightest effect," he says.

Meanwhile, the sensible voice of Chris McGovern, chairman of the Campaign for Real Education, said: "There may be a case for legal action against the school and the BBC if any child has suffered psychological harm or distress, either in the short term or the long term.

"The BBC seems unable to separate fantasy from reality. The fantasy world created at Lanesend Primary School might be permissible in science fiction drama such as Doctor Who, but it can run close to child abuse when translated into real life."

In the programme both sexes felt violated at having gender neutral toilets. Girls said: "I try not to go at school", and "I hold it in all day". Boys were equally appalled.

I ask where were the parents? Why did they agree to this experiment? Why did the school and its governors? Why are we paying people to dream up this monster experimental programme?

Divisive gender politics through school uniforms

In the US they don't have school uniforms. This may work or not. In the UK we feel it is important that all children are dressed to identify pupils of a particular school, to be proud of their uniform, school badge and community and children are not competing for the latest designer gear, it is also cheaper, in most cases.

We do not generally discriminate if a girl wishes to wear trousers but recently schools have felt the need to join the gender race for stupidity.

A headmaster recently banned girls from wearing skirts to accommodate the growing number of transgender pupils and to deal with complaints over the 'decency' of how short skirts are worn.

The headmaster (note the term 'master', because he's a man!): "We know the current uniform is not necessarily worn as respectfully as it should be. There were problems with decency and a number of issues raised by people in the community about how students were wearing uniform."

One mother said: "My daughter and her friends are appalled by this. The school is creating a hostile environment for girls." I agree.

Another parent added: "My daughter said she has got a gender and it's female, so being gender neutral when she has got a gender is a big deal for her, as she proud to be a girl. I feel girls should be allowed to wear skirts if they want to." Good for her, be out and be proud!

Since the 1960s girls have hiked up their skirts to attract boys and make their legs look longer. Along with the illicit wearing of make-up, hairspray and painted nails, we did then and now - we try our still do our best to attract the opposite sex.

People in the community raising issues? I can only think of the Islamic religious nuts who might occupy the same space as these girls would be the only ones to object to short skirts.

Associated Press (AP) had a mad summer of 2017

Reviewing a San Francisco 'Rainbow Day Camp' school to explore transgender:

The AP spoke to "gender experts," who tell parents to allow their sons and daughters to "do a weekend as a different gender."

"How can a parent know if their child is transgender? What separates a young boy who might be transgender from one with a vivid imagination who likes to dress up in his sister's dresses?" the AP asks. "What do you do if your daughter tells you she's a boy?"

The answer, according to the wire service, is "we don't know."

"Do a weekend as a different gender, and see what you learn," a parent said. "People have said this over and over again: "Oh, my God. I saw a side of my child I had never seen before.'"

The conclusion sums it up: "We are definitely seeing more kids socially transitioning at very young ages," she told the AP. "And the reason we're seeing this more is because we're looking for them, and letting them be found."
In my opinion, this is pure child abuse.

Chapter 6

What is the science behind it all and what are the numbers?

Given the importance of imposing transgenderism on the majority, you would think the numbers were huge?

Well they're not and it is unforgivable to waste taxpayers' cash on this and indoctrinating our children's minds.

Gender dysphoria has been reported across many countries and cultures. Among individuals who are assigned male gender at birth, approximately 0.005 percent to 0.014 percent are diagnosed with gender dysphoria. Among individuals who are assigned female gender at birth, approximately 0.002 percent to 0.003 percent are diagnosed with gender dysphoria.

https://www.psychologytoday.com/conditions/gender-dysphoria

A very low figure for a condition that is gaining so much attention and where public policy is doing so much harm.

First do no harm

Dr Kenneth Zucker, was until 2015 the leading expert on transgender children, until his unfashionable and un-PC science led to his being sacked in 2015 from a Toronto gender identity clinic, Centre for Addiction and Mental Health.

Under pressure, those who took the "gender affirmative" view to young people who feel they were born with the wrong gender took hold, which encourages parents to allow their children with gender dysphoria to live as their chosen sex.

He had previously said that his goal was "lowering the odds that as such a kid gets older he or she will move into adolescence feeling so uncomfortable about their gender identity that they think that it would be better to live as the other gender and require treatment with hormones and sex-reassignment surgery".

Activists and psychologist all admit that they are at a precipice in terms of trans rights in the UK. Psychologists also believe youngsters are seven times more likely to be on the autistic spectrum as they fixate on issues, which could convince children they are the wrong sex. Many also believe that the children are gay, rather than trans.

Dr Zucker for 30 years ran Canada's biggest child gender clinic and recognised as an authority on childhood gender dysphoria until he lost his job. He believes he was sacked for challenging the gender affirmative approach. He recommended encouraging parents to allow their children with gender dysphoria to live as their chosen sex. Of course, Zucker's approach was likened to reparative therapy, which had the intended goal of 'curing' children. Alongside this, he advocated more clinical analysis of the underlying psychological and mental health issues associated with children to believe they were born in the wrong gender.

When CAMH sacked Zucker they also walked away from a $1m grant to study the effects of hormone blockers on teenagers. In Canada, these grants are very hard to come by.

More evidence of the insidious campaign of trans rights campaigners to bury the evidence?

This family had used Zucker's services:

When Carol's eldest son was four years old, he would dream he was a girl and sob when he woke up as a boy. Around the same time, two ten-year-old kids threw him off the monkey bars when they saw him playing with a Barbie. He was still bleeding when his mom picked him up. Carol, a Toronto woman who works in education, says she and her husband had always honoured his preferences, for stereotypically "girl" movies, toys and clothes. They had three sons, and they were all different. But the bullying worried them, and school was proving tricky.

So, in late 2007, they went to see Dr. Zucker. After lengthy family interviews and tests, he laid out his recommended treatment. "It was not offensive or cruel to us," recalls Carol, who detailed the family's experience to The Globe and Mail, but asked their identity be protected "It seemed pretty flexible." As Dr. Zucker explained it to Carol, his theory was to help kids value the "body they have." In that case, it meant helping her son see that "you may want to be a girl, but it's okay to be a boy." Carol says she and her husband had only one agenda for their son: "It was 100 per cent about his happiness."

For the next year, they visited the clinic twice a week, and then roughly once a week for nearly three years after that. Their son would have play therapy while Carol and her husband would meet with Dr. Zucker. At home, they slowly took away the dolls and pink toys, with their son choosing which ones. "He would be upset," Carol admits, "and ask for them the next day." But his favourites remained, and the missing toys were replaced with "gender neutral" options, such as Lego and toy animals. "Her son," Carol insists, "never touched a truck unless he tripped over it."

Over time, says Carol, he found common ground with his brothers. He was diagnosed as gifted and received help for attention deficit hyperactivity disorder, after the clinic's assessment diagnosed it. His school situation improved and he made friends. But always, Dr. Zucker cautioned them to resist too much accommodation from his teachers: "Don't let the school make him a poster child," Carol recalls him saying. "Don't let them parade him around for pink assemblies. This is his personal journey and we don't know where he is going to end up."

As Carol saw it, no direction was being prescribed – if her son still wanted to be a girl as he got older, Dr. Zucker said, hormone therapy was an option. "The work we did was centred around the whole idea that they are kind of young to make a decision, and if they are going to want to transition, we will know."

Carol previously spoke about her son's experience for a story on National Public Radio in 2008. The documentary was part of the case submitted to CAMH in January, 2015, by Rainbow Health Ontario, a province-wide organisation that advocates on behalf of the LGBT community. Back then, only a few months into therapy, Carol detailed her son's distress, how he tried to hide his toys and soberly drew pictures of girls for hours. "I think he was really lost ..." she told the radio program.

Carol believes that Dr. Zucker's advice worked for her son, who is now a popular gay 13-year-old. He doesn't talk about wanting to be a girl any more, though Carol says they are careful not assume his path is set. "The biggest and most important thing I hold on to as a mother, was that when he was young, he would never talk about his future, never talk about himself as an adult." Now, she says, he is making plans. "This was a healthy outcome for us." She gives Dr. Zucker the credit: "I know the positive impact his therapy had on the culture of our family."

https://beta.theglobeandmail.com/news/toronto/gender-identity-debate-swirls-over-camh-psychologist-transgender-program/article28758828/?ref=http://www.theglobeandmail.com&

Is there a biological basis for the current craze of trans and is the rise in clinics and treatments justified, at least for our children?

In a liberal left newspaper, Qazi Rahman, a lead investigator into LGBT mental health at King's College, London, '"We know much more about how nature shapes sexual orientation, and my view of the science is that nurture does very little, if any, shaping of sexual orientation. We know next to nothing about how people come to feel transgender."

The proliferation of words used to describe gender identity adds a further complication: scientists need to know if such terms are stable psychological constructs, Rahman says. "That doesn't mean they are not real or important to people, but researchers need to interrogate these constructs more thoroughly to see if they represent a real ground shift, and are connected in some real sense to non-heterosexual or transgender identities."

"How do prenatal sex hormones shape the developing brain circuitry which controls your sense of gender identity? Where is that network? How does it work to make this happen and how does it map out over time, from early childhood to middle childhood through to adolescence and young adulthood? And how does that become different in some people to the sex they were assigned at birth?

"The answer is, we don't know." And that my friends is the big question, so I ask why are our politicians bowing to the very vocal trans lobby groups?

Data on long-term outcomes for trans children are scarce. No one is tracking the evidence on puberty-blocking intervention either.

The doctors involved in this should refer back to their oath, First do no harm.

https://www.theguardian.com/society/2016/jul/10/gender-identity-transgender-science-how-big-questions-unanswered

In the US, the American Psychiatric Association has eliminated sexual identity disorders from its psychiatric diagnoses.

Paul McHugh, formerly psychiatrist-in-chief at Johns Hopkins hospital, continues to state that transgenderism is a mental disorder and that, purely for political and ideological reasons, sufferers are being denied the treatment they need.

Studies show, he has said, that between 70 per cent and 80 per cent of children who express transgender feelings "spontaneously lose those feelings" over time. Even among those satisfied with gender-reassignment surgery, their subsequent "psycho-social adjustments" had not improved.

Dr McHugh lost the argument. As a result California, New Jersey and Massachusetts have passed laws barring psychiatrists, "even with parental permission, from striving to restore natural gender feelings to a transgender minor".

https://www.thetimes.co.uk/article/now-we-all-have-to-live-by-radical-feminist-rules-nfzrh2jtg

Transgender Surgery Isn't the Solution

Fascinating stuff from Dr McHugh, former psychiatrist in chief at John Hopkins Hospital. Written in 2014 and updated in 2016.

Reacting to the US government and media alliance advancing the transgender cause has gone into overdrive in recent weeks. On May 30, a U.S. Department of Health and Human Services review board ruled that Medicare can pay for the "reassignment" surgery sought by the transgendered—those who say that they don't identify with their biological sex. Earlier last month Defense Secretary Chuck Hagel said that he was "open" to lifting a ban on transgender individuals serving in the military. Time magazine, seeing the trend, ran a cover story for its June 9 issue called "The Transgender Tipping Point: America's next civil rights frontier."

Yet policy makers and the media are doing no favours either to the public or the transgendered by treating their confusions as a right in need of defending rather than as a mental disorder that deserves understanding, treatment and prevention. This intensely felt sense of being transgendered constitutes a mental disorder in two respects. The first is that the idea of sex misalignment is simply mistaken—it does not correspond with physical reality. The second is that it can lead to grim psychological outcomes.

The transgendered suffer a disorder of "assumption" like those in other disorders familiar to psychiatrists. With the transgendered, the disordered assumption is that the individual differs from what seems given in nature—namely one's maleness or femaleness. Other kinds of disordered assumptions are held by those who suffer from anorexia and bulimia nervosa, where the assumption that departs from physical reality is the belief by the dangerously thin that they are overweight.

With body dysmorphic disorder, an often socially crippling condition, the individual is consumed by the assumption "I'm ugly." These disorders occur in subjects who have come to believe that some of their psycho-social conflicts or problems will be resolved if they can change the way that they appear to others. Such ideas work like ruling passions in their subjects' minds and tend to be accompanied by a solipsistic argument.

For the transgendered, this argument holds that one's feeling of "gender" is a conscious, subjective sense that, being in one's mind, cannot be questioned by others. The individual often seeks not just society's tolerance of this "personal truth" but affirmation of it. Here rests the support for "transgender equality," the demands for government payment for medical and surgical treatments, and for access to all sex-based public roles and privileges.

With this argument, advocates for the transgendered have persuaded several states—including California, New Jersey and Massachusetts—to pass laws barring psychiatrists, even with parental permission, from striving to restore natural gender feelings to a transgender minor. That government can intrude into parents' rights to seek help in guiding their children indicates how powerful these advocates have become.

How to respond? Psychiatrists obviously must challenge the solipsistic concept that what is in the mind cannot be questioned. Disorders of consciousness, after all, represent psychiatry's domain; declaring them off-limits would eliminate the field. Many will recall how, in the 1990s, an accusation of parental sex abuse of children was deemed unquestionable by the solipsists of the "recovered memory" craze.

You won't hear it from those championing transgender equality, but controlled and follow-up studies reveal fundamental problems with this movement. When children who reported transgender feelings were tracked without medical or surgical treatment at both Vanderbilt University and London's Portman Clinic, 70%-80% of them spontaneously lost those feelings. Some 25% did have persisting feelings; what differentiates those individuals remains to be discerned.

We at Johns Hopkins University—which in the 1960s was the first American medical center to venture into "sex-reassignment surgery"—launched a study in the 1970s comparing the outcomes of transgendered people who had the surgery with the outcomes of those who did not. Most of the surgically treated patients described themselves as "satisfied" by the results, but their subsequent psycho-social adjustments were no better than those who didn't have the surgery. And so at Hopkins we stopped doing sex-reassignment surgery, since producing a "satisfied" but still troubled patient seemed an inadequate reason for surgically amputating normal organs.

It now appears that our long-ago decision was a wise one. A 2011 study at the Karolinska Institute in Sweden produced the most illuminating results yet regarding the transgendered, evidence that should give advocates pause. The long-term study—up to 30 years—followed 324 people who had sex-reassignment surgery. The study revealed that beginning about 10 years after having the surgery, the transgendered began to experience increasing mental difficulties. Most shockingly, their suicide mortality rose almost 20-fold above the comparable non-transgender population. This disturbing result has as yet no explanation but probably reflects the growing sense of isolation reported by the aging transgendered after surgery. The high suicide rate certainly challenges the surgery prescription.

There are subgroups of the transgendered, and for none does "reassignment" seem apt. One group includes male prisoners the convicted national-security leaker who now wishes to be called Chelsea. Facing long sentences and the rigors of a men's prison, they have an obvious motive for wanting to change their sex and hence their prison. Given that they committed their crimes as males, they should be punished as such; after serving their time, they will be free to reconsider their gender.

Another subgroup consists of young men and women susceptible to suggestion from "everything is normal" sex education, amplified by Internet chat groups. These are the transgender subjects most like anorexia nervosa patients: They become persuaded that seeking a drastic physical change will banish their psycho-social problems. "Diversity" counsellors in their schools, rather like cult leaders, may encourage these young people to distance themselves from their families and offer advice on rebutting arguments against having transgender surgery. Treatments here must begin with removing the young person from the suggestive environment and offering a counter-message in family therapy.

Then there is the subgroup of very young, often prepubescent children who notice distinct sex roles in the culture and, exploring how they fit in, begin imitating the opposite sex. Misguided doctors at medical centers including Boston's Children's Hospital have begun trying to treat this behaviour by administering puberty-delaying hormones to render later sex-change surgeries less onerous—even though the drugs stunt the children's growth and risk causing sterility. Given that close to 80% of such children would abandon their confusion and grow naturally into adult life if untreated, these medical interventions come close to child abuse. A better way to help these children: with devoted parenting.

At the heart of the problem is confusion over the nature of the transgendered. "Sex change" is biologically impossible. People who undergo sex-reassignment surgery do not change from men to women or vice versa. Rather, they become feminized men or masculinized women. Claiming that this is civil-rights matter and encouraging surgical intervention is in reality to collaborate with and promote a mental disorder.
https://www.wsj.com/articles/paul-mchugh-transgender-surgery-isnt-the-solution-1402615120

**The British NHS publishes the following advice:
What causes gender dysphoria?**

Gender development is complex and there are many possible variations that cause a mismatch between a person's biological sex and their gender identity, making the exact cause of gender dysphoria unclear.

Occasionally, the hormones that trigger the development of biological sex may not work properly on the brain, reproductive organs and genitals, causing differences between them. This may be caused by:

- additional hormones in the mother's system – possibly as a result of taking medication
- the foetus' insensitivity to the hormones, known as an-

drogen insensitivity syndrome (AIS) – when this happens, gender dysphoria may be caused by hormones not working properly in the womb

Gender dysphoria may also be the result of other rare conditions, such as:

- congenital adrenal hyperplasia (CAH) – where a high level of male hormones are produced in a female foetus. This causes the genitals to become more male in appearance and, in some cases, the baby may be thought to be biologically male when she is born.
- intersex conditions – which cause babies to be born with the genitalia of both sexes (or ambiguous genitalia). Parents are recommended to wait until the child can choose their own gender identity before any surgery is carried out.

How common is gender dysphoria?

It's not known exactly how many people experience gender dysphoria, because many people with the condition never seek help.

A survey of 10,000 people undertaken in 2012 by the Equality and Human Rights Commission found that 1% of the population surveyed was gender variant, to some extent.

While gender dysphoria appears to be rare, the number of people being diagnosed with the condition is increasing, due to growing public awareness.

However, many people with gender dysphoria still face prejudice and misunderstanding.

What is interesting about the above is the admittance that women taking medication (ie contraceptives such as 'the pill') maybe contributing to this recent phenomena. (More in Ch13, Sid Lukkassen)

Additional reading:

https://www.transgendertrend.com/born-in-the-wrong-body/
https://www.transgendertrend.com/professionals-questioning-medical-transition-children/
https://www.transgendertrend.com/alternative-views/

The Fight Back – de-trasitioning, commonsense

Dare not speak thy name - the taboo subject of de-transitioning

In normal society if one makes a mistake you would look to history, case studies and facts to rectify that mistake. Not in the transgender world.

Not often seen in the media and spoken about by trans activists are those who have undergone trans surgery and are now de-transitioning.

There is a fascinating survey conducted by 'Transgender Trend', a UK based group of parents and individuals who are concerned about the current rend to diagnose 'gender non-conforming' children as transgender. They reject current conservative, reactionary, religious fundamentalist views about sexuality and have no political affiliation. They are also concerned about legislation that places transgender rights above the right to safety for girls and young women in public bathrooms and changing rooms.

Good luck to them, you can read more about them here:

https://www.transgendertrend.com/about_us/

Some quotes from their survey into de-transitioning:

'Therapy before surgery – I think people who identify as transgender have a mental illness/social problems (ie misogyny) that needs to be treated with therapy instead of cutting off body parts. Nobody would tell a body dysmorphic person to cut off his leg and make themselves feel better?'

On surgery: '… it didn't for me, as my issue was not being trans, even though both medical professionals and society made me believe it was'.

'It's a mental disorder where the patient is in charge of their treatment while refusing counselling and it really does seem like forcing everyone into elective surgeries and lifelong hormonal treatment is big pharma's answer to transgenderism'.

On trans women, 'I have experienced the trans community up close and personal from the inside. I went into it completely convinced that trans women are just like any other women. After interacting with a great number of them over a long period of time I now know that they are not, and as a group they have very little care for actual women. Every other avenue of treatment should be investigated first.'

'I mostly feel anger at the trans medical system/liberal ideology and concern for people who decide to transition – much of which is informed by my own experiences.'

'While I still experience physical dysphoria from time to time and occasionally desire transition, I find that the risk outweigh the benefits.'

'The only positive outcome for me is that I was able to identify femininity, not womanhood, as my problem and understand that these are separate.'

'It was a childhood/teen phase before I accepted myself as a lesbian as an adult.'

'I used transition as self harm. It destroyed so many parts of my life.'

https://www.transgendertrend.com/about_us/
How has stopping transition impacted your dysphoria?
What led you to stop transition?
Do you believe you were given adequate counselling and accurate information about transition?
Age distribution of transition and detransition

Their survey into de-transitioning can be found here:

https://www.transgendertrend.com/detransition/

Desistance of Trans kids

There is little data on de-transitioning, however, there has been almost a dozen studies of looking at the rate of "desistance," among trans-identified kids—which, in this context, refers to cases in which trans kids eventually identify as their sex at birth. Canadian sex researcher James Cantor summarized those studies' findings **in a blog post**: "Despite the differences in country, culture, decade, and follow-up length and method, all the studies have come to a remarkably similar conclusion:

Only very few trans-kids still want to transition by the time they are adults. Instead, they generally turn out to be regular gay or lesbian folks." The exact rate of desistance varied by study, but overall, they concluded that about 80% of trans kids eventually identified as their sex at birth. Some trans activists and academics, however, argue that these studies are flawed, the patients surveyed weren't really transgender, and that mass desistance doesn't exist. Of course they argue against this, it's an industry that comes with cash and media kudos.

That is why the trans lobbyists are so dangerous.

UK University bans research into transgender reverse surgery

The debate is being shut down.

Recently James Caspian, a psychotherapist researcher was refused permission to conduct a study into cases of people who have had surgery to reverse gender reassignment because they were afraid of a social media backlash.

The university gave little explanation other than that it was "politically incorrect" research and had the potential for an online campaign that "may be detrimental to the reputation of the institution".

Mr Caspian, a counsellor who specialises in therapy for transgender people, wanted to conduct the research after a surgeon who carries out reverse trans surgery said that people are regretting their decisions.

He specifically wanted to study women who had transed to men and reverted to living as a woman but without the reverse surgery.

It is stunning that a British university is shutting down debate and going against the basic tenets of academic and intellectual freedom, whilst we are supposed to accept that transgender should be taught in our primary schools and accepted in corporate life, yet academics in the field are stopped from questioning a very legitimate and pressing question of reversal and its impact.

In 2017 in Australia, another teen named Patrick, who had begun taking puberty blockers, said he had ceased taking the drugs after changing his mind and deciding to remain male.

All the experts agree that prescribing puberty-blockers for young people is an experimental treatment, unsupported by rigorous scientific evidence.

Another doctor, a world leading genital reconstructive surgeon, Professor Miroslaw Djordjevic, is speaking out.

Around five years ago he was contacted at his Belgrade clinic to perform a so-called gender reassignment 'reversal' surgery. Over the following six months another six people had also approached him. They came from all over the Western world, united by a sense of regret.

Re-attaching male genitalia is a very complex and costly (€18k) and takes several operations over a year to fully complete.

He said those wishing to reverse their operations have spoken to him about experiencing crippling levels of depression following transition and thoughts of suicide, yet the industry is brushing it under the carpet.

He has real concerns about the level of psychiatric evaluation and counselling people receive in other clinics before surgery takes place.

To date, all of his reversals have been transgender women aged over 30 wanting to restore their male genitalia. Over the last two decades, the average age of his patients has more than halved, from 45 years old to 21. While the World Professional Association for Transgender Health guidelines currently state nobody under the age of 18 should undergo surgery, Prof Djordjevic fears this age limit could soon be reduced to include minors. And it will because of the violent campaigns in the trans world.

Were that to happen, he says, he would refuse to abide by the rules. "I'm afraid what will happen five to 10 years later with this person," he says. "It is more than about surgery; it's an issue of human rights. I could not accept them as a patient because I'd be afraid what would happen to their brain and mind." He's right, but whose human rights? We have a duty to protect our young and vulnerable.

He has deep reservations about treating children with drugs before they reach puberty.

Nevertheless, he is still part of an industry where the debate is being shut down. We need more conversation and evidence.

http://www.telegraph.co.uk/health-fitness/body/gender-reversal-surgery-rise-arent-talking/

The sad lives of children that end in death

As the debate and hormones are handed out the under reported – because we just don't know about them – are the children who are at higher risk of depression, self-harm and suicide.

In 2017 an inquest heard how a 15-year-old boy, Leo Etherington, who was born female, had hanged himself in his bedroom. The teenager had been the first young person to publicly reveal at the age of 12 that he had started receiving puberty blocking injections. He, sadly, will not be the last.

Gay? What do you make of 'conversion therapy'?

I often take part in a BBC radio phone-in on various subjects. The BBC station is in my county of Kent, UK where controversial subjects are discussed. Recently, following the prime minister's condemnation of 'gay conversion therapy', which is growing in the UK, they asked listeners their opinion.

"Conversion therapy" is a "treatment" which aims to reduce or stop same-sex attraction or suppress a person's gender identity. It was until 2015 offered on the NHS. It is not banned (for now).

Whether you believe in this practice or not, it is not illegal. The BBC published an online poll inviting people to give their views, asking 'should gay conversion be banned?'. This was after a doctor had warned that 'gay therapy is akin to psychological abuse'.

The poll by the BBC sparked 'outrage' on social media (according to left leaning MSM), with the BBC issuing three apologies on Twitter.

I took a look at the 'opinions'. It was tweeted via a gay link and that's when the 'outrage' happened. Idiots were tweeting whether racism should be banned (it is), or 'is torture ok' (it's banned). Others joked it would be good to be gay. It is all very banal.

I am not going to go into the pros or cons of the therapy, if there are any, my point is about free speech on a practice that is, for now, legal. My enemies often claim I voted against gay conversion therapy. Not true, I always vote against the EU interfering in others' lives.

Whatever happened to opinions and discussion?

The annual number of referrals to the gender dysphoria specialist team at the Astrid Lindgren Children's Hospital in Stockholm. Referenced article in Swedish:

http://lakartidningen.se/Klinik-och-vetenskap/Klinisk-oversikt/2017/02/Kraftig-okning-av-konsdysfori-bland-barn-och-unga/ …

"A Different Stripe", Renee Sullivan, Psychology Today, 2018

https://www.psychologytoday.com/articles/201803/different-stripe

It's been four years since I reidentified as a woman. My gender dysphoria was real and often painful, but the way for me to resolve it wasn't by becoming a man. It was by questioning and rejecting the stories society had told me about what it means to be a woman.

Some charts illustrating the steadily increasing number of natal females presenting to gender clinics, worldwide.

Minority issues are taking over – or are they – or is it just this decade's decadence? From fat issues to global warming

Why are we bending over backwards so that extreme minorities have safe spaces that are invading the spaces of the rest of us?

A small minority of people have extreme eating disorders, bulimia, where body dysmorphic disorder (estimates have been put at 1:100) but are we under pressure from the bulimic industry to remove mirrors in public bathrooms, have separate eating areas in staff and school canteens or have this issue greeting us in school reception areas or in every facet of public life or education curricula?

And they have an industry – publicly funded programmes through hospitals and GP practices, private clinics and it is a medically recognised health problem, with mental illness issues. But is it pushed down our throats (pardon the pun)?

Yet we don't see their supporters or the victims of this illness marching on the White House or the UK Parliament, demanding that the rest of us eat privately or that mirrors throughout the land should be destroyed.

However, there is a growing anti-fat shaming body that looms large (together with their lardy arses) who believe they have to right to stuff as much food and drink into their mouths and expect the rest of us to pick up the tab for their over indulgence in public health costs and having to sit next to one on an aeroplane. If they are too fat to fit into an ordinary seat they should be made to pay more so that they can expand hips, thigh and backsides into the seat beside them and pay their fair share of fuel to get them into the air.

Then there are the man-made climate change deniers (blasphemers). Anyone who questions the wisdom of the second coming on this – Al Gore – who practically created the industry and made millions out of it – are labelled lunatics and heretics.

Any scientist looking to balance the argument or who provides alternative science facts is drummed out of their university, publicly denounced and stripped of all funding and professional dignity.

Our kids are told their science is real and the world – the world they will inherit – is at risk and therefore green taxes must be levied, cars are bad, farming practices are bad, extreme weather is the result of man-made global warming. Man is bad, your parents are bad, government is good, high green taxation is good.

I have had many university students visit the European Parliament when, on a Q&A session, have challenged my stance on global warming. They are genuinely shocked when I challenge the educational Marxism they have suffered as they have never been taught to examine the other side of the argument. It doesn't exist in their curriculum.

A professor of psychology at the University of Toronto, Jordan Peterson, has been under attack from the right-on crowd, his job at the university is under threat because of his very vocal and reasonable views. With two written warnings he has also faced the transgender militia.

He has an enormous online presence – his videos on YouTube have had 150 million views.

Last year he was briefly suspended from YouTube and Google without explanation.

What has he done wrong? Is he a paedophile, a dangerous sexual deviant, a sexual predator, a rapist? No, just a professor because he refuses to use the preferred gender pronouns of radical transgender activists.

After all, he's a professor of psychology, isn't debate and analysis what they do? No, because he's breaking Canadian law. He dislikes the fact that the state is dictating his thought process, calling it …'ceding linguistic territory to post-modernist neo-Marxists'.

He self identifies as a classic British liberal, infuriating the left and right in equal measures.

Like many, he disagrees that gender is a social construct and is a biological fact. He believes our male children are being undermined at every level of education, making them question their worth to society and whether they can achieve.

Speaking to the British Spectator magazine he slams universities for their illiberal and unscientific thinking: "The humanities in the universities have become almost incomprehensively shallow and corrupt in multiple ways, ... they don't rely on science because they are not scientifically educated. This is try particularly in sociology, where they mask their complete ignorance of sciences by claiming that science is just another mode of knowing and that it's only privileged within the structure of the oppressive Eurocentric patriarchy. It's appalling, we're not having an intelligent conversation, we are having an ideological conversation." The writer, Tim Lott, goes on to say that he is one of the most important thinkers to emerge on the world stage for many years but fears whether 'he will be destroyed by the forces that oppose him'.

And that's our dilemma. Do we let people like Peterson get sacked for his sentientious views or, if we agree with him, and many do, we need to stand up for his right to thoughtful speech, against the fascism that is trying to shut him down.

Governments have to think whether the humanities departments are contributing to or undermining our free thinking and free will. Billions are pumped into gender studies, cultural studies, gender and sexuality, and all linked to racism, cultural reproduction, sexual diversities and a photography course thrown in for fun (York University). Are these courses a costly exercise in infecting young people's minds to be challenged to turn against us and in turn unleashed to undermine the fabric of society? Is this a good use of taxpayers' cash? As our governments evidently think they are – and saddling kids with years of student debt – perhaps their courses should also include compulsory lessons in science.

Shutting down debate with well-funded extremist arguments seems to be winning the day.

Chapter 7

Trans facts and figures from around the world

Whilst we on the right valiantly fight against the culture wars that are raging in the UK, EU and US, it is worth a little reality check pinch here, we are not alone.

Let's take a look at the numbers of trans people in the UK, US and EU and ponder why our children are being brainwashed.

The UK

A UK charity, the gender identity charity Gires, says even the most conservative estimate in these studies – 0.2% – would suggest there are 130,000 people in the UK who feel gender incongruent enough to seek medical intervention, such as cross-sex hormones and surgery. The vast majority have yet to present for treatment.

In figures:

15,000 trans patients
Roughly 12,700 adults and 2,700 children
5,714 people changed passports in 2015

When you consider that trans make up less than 1% of the population, there is an inordinate amount of money, laws and time taken up with this marginal subject.

The EU (in Europe more widely)

Legal Gender Recognition (for public documents & legal affairs) exists in 35 European countries (EU has 27 member states, exc UK) but not in 14 others.

Only 12 states in Europe protect against transphobic violence:

Where figures are available, 1% of people identifying as transgender are small, yet so much money and publicity is attached to their agenda.

Belgium, The Netherlands and New Zealand.

Interestingly some countries require sterilisation for transitioning, where it is compulsory for change of gender in:

Austria; Denmark; Finland; France; Ukraine; Luxembourg; Romania & France.

However, it is not required in:

Spain; UK; Sweden; Portugal; Hungary; Italy & Germany. These countries are seeing trans women, living as men, who are having babies.

Attitudes differ in conservative and catholic countries.

Spain

In Spain there seems to be a generational effect with people between 14-29 being much more willing to be open about their condition (14%) compared to older people.

Individuals who identify as transgender are allowed to change their legal gender without the need of sex reassignment surgery or sterilisation. Discrimination regarding sexual orientation and gender identity and expression has been banned nationwide since 1996.

Hungary

Hungry is getting itself into all manner of arguments in the EU: border control, forced migrant quotes and sexuality.

According to a 2012 poll by the European Union Agency for Fundamental Rights 45% of the Hungarian LGBTQI respondents have personally felt discriminated against or harassed on the grounds of sexual orientation in the last 12 months, and 46% of trans respondent on grounds of trans status.

Trans people are twice as likely to report experiencing discrimination at work than non-trans gays and lesbians (29% vs. 15%). They are also more likely to have experienced long-term unemployment in the past 5 years (46% vs. 27%).

Diagnosis of transsexualism and change of legal gender is mandatory for trans specific health care. Health insurance covers only 10% of the costs of gender reassignment surgeries. The lack of specialised surgeons in the public health care system is also a huge obstacle. (ECRI)

Poland

Poland is a deeply conservative and traditional country. Again in conflict with the EU over borders, forced migrant quotas and also sexuality.

In 2013, former President and Nobel prize winner Lech Wałęsa said that gay MPs should sit at the back of the parliament or even behind a wall and should not have important positions in Parliament. The former President also stated that minorities should not impose themselves upon the majority. Wałęsa could not have been accused of inciting to hatred because the Polish penal code doesn't include inciting to hatred against sexual orientation

Denmark

In February 2013, a Guatemalan became the first transgender person to be granted asylum in Denmark because of persecution in her native country.[1] However, she was put in a facility for men, where she had been assaulted several times and was initially refused. They reopened the case when LGBT Denmark proved her life would be in danger if she returned to Guatemala.

In June 2014, the Danish parliament voted 59-52 to remove the requirement of diagnosis with a mental disorder and surgery with irreversible sterilization during the process of a legal sex change. This makes Denmark the first European country to remove the Gender Identity Disorder diagnosis as a necessary requirement in the gender recognition process. Since 1 September 2014, Danes over 18 years old who wish to apply for a legal sex change can do so by stating that they want to change their documentation, followed by a six-month-long "reflection period" to confirm the request.

In September 2014, a law went into effect in Denmark effectively dropping the former practice of requiring transgender persons to undergo arduous psychiatric evaluation and castration before being allowed legal gender change. By requiring nothing more than a statement of gender identity and subsequent confirmation of the request for gender change after a waiting period of 6 months, this means that anyone wishing their legal gender marker changed can do so with no expert-evaluation and few other formal restrictions.

Pending a decision by the World Health Organization to remove transgender gender identity from its list of mental illnesses, Denmark initially postponed a unilateral change. Citing a lack of progress at the WHO, the Danish parliament decided to remove transgender gender identity from the National Board of Health's list of mental illnesses in 2016. The change came into effect on 1 January 2017. It was the second European country to do this, after France which introduced a similar legislation in 2010 under a so-called conservative, Nicolas Sarkozy (more reform too place under hard left socialist, President Hollande).

Norway

Meanwhile, Norwegian Health Minister Bent Høie has made promises that a similar law, as Denmark, for Norway will be drafted soon.

Sweden

In 1972, Sweden became the first country in the world to allow people who were transsexual by legislation to surgically change their sex and provide free hormone replacement therapy.

Meanwhile in Sweden ... 'transgendered men are not real men' and migrants

According to the wonderful Breitbart UK, transgender activists attacked Sweden's first women-only festival for only banning biological men, as this could imply transgendered men are not real men.

A comedian set up a music festival as women only because of the mass sexual attacks at other festivals, largely committed to migrants. (My US readers may recall President Trump referring to this and was then shot down by the main stream media?). All over Europe, and in particular Sweden, women are being attacked by migrants. In July 2016 they, apparently attacked nearly 40 women, including five rapes, at Sweden's largest music festival.

Again, in true Monty Python style, questions were asked about how they would define 'men'. The organisers responded – in truly mad gender neutral style – that only 'cis' men would be banned (readers, that's men who were born male and still identify as male, while they still can).

The row soon widened. What do you do with men who are vulnerable and oppressed, then? Homosexual men, non-white men? Are they welcome? Why only cis men and not just men? Are transgender less male?

Whether the Judean People's Front concert will go ahead or will it be hi-jacked by the People's Front of Judea, isn't yet clear.

Italy

There is no specific mention of transgender people – they are included in LGBT figures.

USA

In the US, 0.3% of the population identifies as trans.

103,813	New York State
163,960	Florida
212,200	Texas
378,513	California

The Left will argue that the above is discriminatory – and some of it is – but at least some of these countries and individuals are fighting for their beliefs. In the corridors of DC, London and the EU there are deranged individuals, swayed by extremist lobby groups who would like to see us all homogenised, lobotomised and a politically correct chip inserted into our brains.

Australia

Australia: Vegan cafe charges 18 percent 'man tax' to fight inequality. "The cafe owner, Alex O'Brien, who describes herself as *"a feminist, not the fun kind,"* told Seven News that the gender tax is only added one week out of every month, and that it's not compulsory. *"If people aren't comfortable pay-*

ing it or if men don't want to pay it, we're not going to kick them out the door," she said.

The 18 percent figure comes from a 2016 Australian government Workplace Gender Equality Agency report which showed women in Australia earn 82 percent of what men do on a yearly basis.

"I had a woman bring her daughters in today and when she came up to the till and saw our gorgeous vulva stones and our period sticker packs she beamed, thanked us for what we were doing and said 'what a beautiful place to take my daughters,'" O'Brien wrote on Facebook. *"We've had men travel across town to visit us and pay 'the man tax' and throw some extra in the donation jar – guys, you're pretty neat."*

The culture wars are being fought but I am not sure yet who will win.

Chapter 8

In the mad, bad world of gender division and diversity

A modern timeline of Gay - LGBT - to LGBTQi and onwards ...

UK Gay rights timeline

- 1967 - Private homosexual acts between men aged over 21 decriminalised in England and Wales

- Blair's 1997 cabinet included Britain's first openly gay minister, they set about immediately bringing down the consent for homosexual sex down from 18 to 16 in 2000

- 1980 - Homosexuality decriminalised in Scotland, then in Northern Ireland in 1982, and in the Isle of Man in 1992

- 1994 - Age of consent for gay men lowered from 21 to 18. It was lowered to 16 in 2001

- 1995 – Gender mainstreaming formally adopted at UN World Conference on Women in Beijing

- 1997 – Gender mainstreaming adopted in EU in Treaty of Amsterdam

- 2000 - Ban on openly gay members of the armed forces lifted

- 2004 – The Gender Recognition Act

- 2005 - Civil partnerships come into effect in the UK. Although until 2010 it was forbidden for civil partnerships to take place in religious institutions

- 2010 – Equality Act

- 2014 - Same-sex marriage laws come into effect in England, Wales and Scotland

- 2015 - Republic of Ireland votes to legalise same-sex marriage

Civil partnerships were introduced in 2005 Across the UK, hundreds of gay and lesbian couples were granted many of the same legal and civil rights as married heterosexuals, albeit with a few outstanding differences around issues such as pensions in the private sector.

Couples could no longer be kept out of hospital rooms where their partner lay dying. They would no longer lose their home or business because of unjust tax laws and they had parental rights over children.

By 2015, more than 138,000 people had a civil partnership - with more than 18,000 people joining in marriage since the Marriage (Same Sex Couples) Act 2013 came into force in England and Wales in March 2014 and in Scotland in December of that year.

But it hasn't been plain sailing

Stonewall, the gay rights campaign group, came under fire in 2010 when they debated over gay marriage and again over whether they supported 'trans people'. They cited that they had to consult with their community. They finally caved in in 2015 to include 'trans equality'.

You can see a pattern here. Marginal until Obama, Blair and EU had their coming out moments and imposed it on the rest of us.

Three examples of what the liberal Left have spawned:

The war of the roses

Recently, a massive punch-up broke out between transgender activists and their extreme feminist rivals.

It's not all plain sailing in the lib/left world of sexual identity. Last summer 'Trans-exclusionary Radical Feminists, aka as TERFs (no, me neither) clashed with their apparent enemies, the 'Members of Action for Trans Health', ATH.

What were they getting their knickers in a twist about?

The alt-left violence of race and anti-conservatism has raised its ugly head in the world of gender rows.

The TERF ladies are feminists opposed to some campaigning by transgender women ATH, although I am not sure whether the trans women are actually women or lads who have transed. Keeping up?

The TERFs, who had organised a meeting to discuss their points were attacked online by ATH. Fearing physical attack, they changed their meeting venue to that venerable public space of free speech, London's Speakers' Corner, in Hyde Park.

When one of their number, a Dr Julia Long, a lesbian feminist, started to sing a song – with a megaphone (?) – the TAs started shouting, 'When the TERFs attack, we fight back'.

The girl on girl action got quite nasty, apparently, with cameras being smashed, punches thrown and the police getting called. Six police officers arrived and, despite the violence, no arrests were made. Surely this is a hate crime? Against who I'm not quite sure. However, the ladies then retired to another venue only to be surrounded again, the staff of the venue had to form a human chain to let the TERFs in.

Subsequently, they have been quite poisonous on social media and have publicly supported violence against women. These lovely ladies are feted by the UK's influential parliamentary committee which studies these things. They are so influential in the political sphere that the committee's report recommended updating legislation to allow "self-declaration" of gender identity and to "de-medicalise" it, which has now found its way to the second part of the legislative process – a consultation. It is half way to becoming law.

These extremists use social media to intimidate their opposition: "punching TERFs is the same as punching Nazis. Fascism must be smashed with the greatest violence to ensure our collective liberation from it … violence against TERFs is always self-defence." The trouble with espousing this nonsense is that it undermines the use of the word 'Nazi' and the atrocities they committed. Do these mad women really think that opposition to people self-declaring their sexuality is Fascism? That's the problem with the extreme left, they do not see that their violent actions are really quite similar to fascism. Fascists hate free speech, dissent, political discourse and academic debate.

These confused darlings believe that anyone who self-identifies as a woman, even without undergoing transition surgery, should be allowed to use women only spaces such as toilets and changing rooms.

You will be happy to hear, however, that a spokesperson for the ATH said: 'We condemn violence against women in all forms. We're proud that many self-organising activists, allies and supporters stood against hatred, misogyny and intimidation.' Mmmmm.

Speakers' Corner has been home to free speech from many around the world for many years. I don't object to people espousing their views, however odd. We must stand up for free speech in our countries because it is frequently under threat. Yet we have to put up with their violence without arrests and our very stretched police service being subjected to intervening in what is reminiscent of a Monty Python film.

Ria, a girl, born a boy named Brad, stopped transitioning at 18 but now wants to be a woman, UK's youngest sex-swap patient

Ria is about to go under the knife for the third time.

Ria, born a boy called Brad, but at 15-years-old, realised she had identified as a girl and was Britain's youngest sex-swap patient.

Having become swamped by the new life, he/she felt scared and may never be accepted as a woman. So he/she stopped treatment just before the surgery and became Brad again.

Keeping up dear readers?

Now he/she is living as a woman and at age 23 years is, apparently, ready to finish the treatment.

'I've always known I was female - it was everyone else who was confused, not me.' That's alright then.

Yet Ms Confused hopes to become a mother. I hope he/she doesn't as we are just storing up more social problems for any child that is put in his/her care. Perhaps he'll freeze his own sperm before his vas deferens are cut out?

http://www.dailymail.co.uk/news/article-4764630/Britain-s-youngest-sex-swap-patient-reassignment.html

Which leads me onto ...

A transgender man (woman who kept her womb) has given birth to a healthy baby boy called Leo.

Trystan Reese, from Portland in Oregon, was born female but started taking hormones nearly 10 years ago.

"I never wanted to change my body," said Mr Reese.
"I never felt like I needed to change my body. And I for sure do not hate my body.

"I feel like my body is awesome and that it is a gift to have been born with the body that I did, and I made the necessary changes so that I could keep living in it," he added.

http://news.sky.com/story/transgender-man-trystan-reese-gives-birth-to-healthy-baby-boy-10972616

Read more at http://talkradio.co.uk/news/kellie-maloney-if-government-says-you-can-wake-and-change-gender-thats-totally-wrong#jIMrsOW2jeYLcUCh.99

These are just a few examples of where this trans issue has led us to.

It is worth noting the speed in which this gender/trans agenda has been forced upon us.

Who asked us? Who voted for it?

Chapter 9

Feminazism and Fighting Back

Why do women on the Right represent what women want better than the feminazis and the Left?

The right stands up for women's rights, whilst the Left is still stuck examining its 1980s dogma.

Gender and 'rights' has become yet another political weapon with the feminazi and trans activists coming from the alt-left. They resort to intimidation and violence, often against those that would have some sympathy with them. And we on the right are fighting back.

Prominent women of the right are taking control of politics in the West, rising fast in new parties and effectively becoming the opposition or at least driving the political agenda for all parties.

Marine Le Pen in France – 11 million votes in 2017 and 35% of the vote Alice Wiedal in Germany, her party, the Alternative for Germany, 3_{rd} largest party Pia Kjærsgaard until recently led the Danish People's Party, the largest party Pernille Vermund, Denmark, leader New Conservatives, rising in popularity Siv Jensen (Progress Party, Norway's minister of finance, with Erna Solberg, prime minister (Conservative)

And we got here without gender quotas

The women on the Right have quietly been marching into power and without a gender quota in sight. The British Labour party and the Greens have had female gender quotas for almost two decades but Labour has still not managed to elect a female leader. The Greens only managed it by changing the rules and the new leader 'job shares' with a man.

In the European Parliament the socialists looks more women friendly as it has managed to select women because of gender quotas. On the other side of the house, Ukip had nearly one third of women elected, selected by the membership of the party, not through gender selection.

Indeed, I was selected by the Ukip membership as the top third person on the MEP list, only Farage and his deputy were ahead of me. The women in Ukip were selected and elected because they were good, not because they were women.

With Nigel Farage standing down, the UKIP membership elected a woman, Diane James, albeit for a short time. Indeed, the top two candidates in the election were women. And in their second selection one of the front runners is a woman. Busting the myth again that the Right is a male dominated world.

Margaret Thatcher was my inspiration for going into politics and Theresa May helped me get where I am today. I helped women in Ukip try to achieve their goals by training and professionalising the party, using what I learned in the Conservative party under May's Women to Win programme. It enabled women to have access to training in public speaking; mentoring; presentation skills; campaigning; how to get selected and provide a support network by women MPs.

Feminism was an issue in the 1970s. They were right to push that agenda. We have achieved equality and have equal pay legislation in place. That legislation just needs to be enforced.

Feminism in the European Parliament, however, follows an extreme agenda. It is obsessed with political correctness, LGBT issues, pushing through abortion rights and gay marriage on former communist countries that are deeply entrenched in Catholicism (and I speak as someone who champions a woman's right to choose and as someone with no faith).

They demand budgets and legislation to ensure that their agenda is pushed through every committee so that all decision are made with LGBT and gender issue consideration. They attempt to push through a gender-specific agenda, instead of a more sensible gender-neutral outlook on politics and society.

Who campaigns for women's rights?

The Left are obsessed with gender quotas; LGBT issues; fighting for women's rights in Muslim countries but ignoring the position of our European female Muslims. They are being abused; undereducated; the victims of female mutilation (FGM); denied language skills and have arranged marriages imposed upon them. They also ignore the victims of paedophile child abuse, instead covering up in government these crimes, committed overwhelmingly by Pakistani heritage men, because the truth is too frightening to admit. Social workers were told to ignore the female victims because they were so frightened of being called racist, instead they focused on the victims as cheap slappers, often in social care and therefore needy girls.

It took a right wing MEP to raise the issue of the child sexual abuse by Muslim men in Rotherham in the UK who lost a law suit against because of her campaign.

Indeed, FGM is only discussed in hush tones. Despite around 500,000 cases of FGM reported in the UK, there has been one prosecution so far. The only reference we make to this is the 'education' of women taking their daughters 'on holiday' to their home states to be mutilated in the name of religion.

Calls for inspections of girls from backgrounds practicing this barbarism is called out for being invasive.

While the Left claims to champion women's rights, in reality they turn a deaf ear to issues that involve migrants, uncomfortable discussing the inconvenient truths within these communities.

It is the Right who raise these issues in the Parliament: the migrant sexual attacks in Cologne, Malmo and in numerous EU cities against Western women. It was scandalous that the left wing media, in collusion with the police, suppressed the attacks so as not to cause offence. As a result women fall victim twice: first in the hands of migrant perpetrators and then by the political correctness of the establishment that tries to sweep atrocities under the carpet. Women are sacrificed for the sake of staying politically correct.

Tolerant Western and pro-migrant citizens started to see the trouble that mass migration by largely uneducated, Arab speaking men caused. It is a clash of civilizations that is left unchecked and even worsened by the European Parliament and Angela Merkel.

When the Right raises these points in debates in Parliament we are shot down by the Left who do not wish to name those involved. Descriptions such as 'Muslim', 'Arab', 'migrants', 'refugees' are never used by the Left, instead in the aftermath of the Paris and Brussels terrorist attacks, it was 'home grown terrorists' that were the problem. Not the fact that they had been radicalised under their noses - that was the fault of everyone else because they were 'marginalised', 'left behind', 'didn't feel included in society'. It was never the fault of their parents, ISIS, radical Islam, their foul hate preachers, the Left always make excuses, never accuses. No wonder female voters are deserting them.

When we suggested that mass migration, open borders and the Schengen free movement of people across the EU were to blame for radicals slipping through to our cities, we were again accused of inciting hatred and ridiculed for questioning one of the essential pillars of the EU - open borders.

They turned their eyes and ears against evidence from police, the armed forces, counter terrorism experts that the migration tsunami would allow terrorists to slip through unnoticed. Unfortunately, we were right and they were wrong. An EU report recently cited there were around 50,000 jihadis in Europe, waiting to strike.

In Britain, the recent bombings were committed by 'child refugees', generously taken in by my country, housed with loving foster parents, paid for by the British taxpayers, given an education and privileges our own British born working classes can only dream of. Yet the left are still in denial. Over half of these supposedly child refugees were over the age of 25.

I was at a 'gender' breakfast one morning when two female Commissioners were urged by a female Labour politician to encourage, through their briefs (read legislation), lone migrant women to work, learn their host country's language and educate their female children. All very laudable and something I would usually agree with. (The men had either been separated from them in their migrant journey or the men were had sent them ahead to claim asylum). This causes two problems when eventually the women and husbands are re-united. The wife and daughters are now educated, presumably integrated and are working. I pointed out the pitfalls. The men are often uneducated, do not speak European languages and their women have been homemakers, not workers and were never likely to be. There is then a clash of civilisations; marriage difficulties; possible domestic violence and abandonment. The Left never think through the consequences of their actions in their quest to 'liberate' women and girls.

My other point at the FEMM breakfast was about tackling multi-culturalism at home. We have 190,000 women in the

UK who do not speak English. We have thousands of women who came to live in the UK forty/fifty years ago who had to learn English to get by. Yet, by the time their own daughters were in their thirties they had forgotten how to speak English because they didn't have to. That's the real crime of the Left as their soft approach caused the women´s isolation and an integration catastrophe

For how are these women and those newly arrived supposed to stop the radicalisation of their children, or help them at school, if they cannot speak or read English?

Who is standing up for Western tolerance, democracy, the rule of law, equal rights, secularism, equality, free speech and our values? It is not the Left but right wing politicians, notably Marine Le Pen and her many female MEPs, Alice Wiedal, Ukip's Margot Parker, Vicky Maier of the PVV, Kristina Winberg of the Swedish Democrats, the women of Austria's FPO and Mara Bizotto of the Lega Nord and myself.

We are accused of hi-jacking gender issues and being opportunistic, as one left wing commentator said,

"They defend 'our' women against harassment by foreigners — strangers, migrants, Muslim men," says Ms. Wodak, the author of "The Politics of Fear: What Right-Wing Populist Discourses Mean." "However, they never spoke out against sexual harassment before."

That's because we have never experienced the extremely high numbers of attacks before mass immigration from Muslim countries who do not respect women.

Marine Le Pen, "It's tough for any female politician, it's never easy, I tell myself to keep going, but it's tough for children, but this is what I believe I have to do. I like to think that I'm doing this for my kids, for other people's kids, too, so they can live in a better society, but, yes, a part of me would rather be at home." She speaks for all of us in politics.

If your name is Le Pen you're the devil in heels, if your name is Mussolini you're the sexy blond with the pumped-up lips

The hatred levelled at Marine Le Pen is a nasty spectacle. She threw her own father out of her party, he said she should disown his name. In every British interview during the presidential campaign the journalists sneakily said they wanted to know about the woman, her politics, her stance on certain issues. But they always interviewed her father too. He dominated the pages, not Marine. Can you ever shake off your family's sins? Yes, if you are called Alessandra Mussolini.

Benito Mussolini's daughter sits in Merkel's EPP group in the European Parliament, she is an MEP of Silvio Berlusconi's Forza Italia, centre right party.

I may find old man Le Pen's views pretty awful and I find Mussolini's fascist dictatorship equally as bad. His granddaughter has said some pretty awful things about faggots, Romanians and French wives of presidents.

Does it take one generation removed to absolve you from your family's sins or is it just the populist right, when they come close to power and influence, that they have to be stopped?

An insight into the workings of the politically correct Parliamentary committees

Feminist ideology and the role of women

As a result of women's exclusion in the West, the second generation of feminist movements that campaigned for legal and social equality for women in the 1960's, represented part of the solution in an attempt to reach a limited equality between men and women. The third (current) wave since the 1990's is what the feminists see as the continuation of the failures of the second wave, yet all we need is the lawmakers to enforce the law. We are equal, implement it!

As part of the third wave of feminism, the gender equality supporters in the European Parliament, the majority of the MEPs in the Women's Right and Gender Equality Committee (FEMM), do not accept the physical characteristics of men and women. Therefore they argue that the "difference" is a mere synonym of "domination and hierarchy". According to them "the gender" is nothing else, but a constructed cultural source of injustice. For example, motherhood is viewed as a form of discrimination instead of being one example of a natural condition of the female state.$_3$

In Western society, feminists believe women can have it all at the same time - career, children and that employers must fit in with their lifestyles rather than business needs.

---

3   In the European Institution "gender equality" is interpreted as being no longer man and woman but neutral human beings with a fluid gender identity.

A friend of mine runs an aesthetics clinic with specialist nurses and beauty therapy practitioners, trained in specialised equipment. She employs ten women, at one point she had half of her staff absent on maternity leave. She could not recruit specialised temporary staff; she could not service her clients; she had extreme cash flow problems which meant her clinic nearly closed.

If you work in sales and you take extended maternity leave, can you honestly pick up where you left with your sales chain and contacts?

If you work in investment banking, can you just walk off the desk during trading to fetch your son from work or job share? You are paid on your performance and skill, not a jobshare.

If you work in a supermarket, the low skilled sector or in a large corporation there maybe some slack, but not in your local specialised market place.

Some women choose to work part-time to fit in with their lifestyle. Some men choose to stay at home, it's pure economics.

Who is standing up for our Judaeo/Christian heritage?

Again, it is the women of the Right. The Left refer to Burkini and burka bans as intolerant, yet in a recent UK poll, a ban was supported by the public by two to one$_1$.

Burkinis and burkas are contradictory to the values of our countries, as they are symbols of oppression and mysogny. It is no coincidence that in the most radical Muslim societies women are forced to wear these garments. Why are we, in Western society, supposed to support these symbols of oppression, contradicting everything we stand for?

The burkini is an Islamacist uniform.

The Left obsess for the minorities who do not wish to uphold our values and choose to cut themselves off from the society in which they have chosen to live.

All we ask is that if you have chosen a Western country in which to live and where you educate your children, that you abide by our laws (and embrace our core values). Yet they wish to live in isolation. This breeds contempt and anger when the jihadis strike. In some parts of London is could be renamed Londonistan (after Pakistan), where, because of uncontrolled immigration, failed family unification policies and a complete disregard for community cohesion, whole swathes of London (and other major cities) are now populated by people who do not mix with white Christians because they do not have to – work, shopping, education is separate and Muslim. Schools are totally Muslim, shops and work too – English doesn't have to be spoken. Where their women are veiled and kept at home.

France is a secular country, very liberal and cultured. Yet they were bombed. They have a far worse non-integration and jihadi problem.

The UK is home to three million Muslims, yet we were bombed. Also bear in mind that half of the three million were born outside of Britain and the numbers have jumped seventy five per cent in ten years.

Germany and Sweden are open, tolerant and liberal, yet their women are raped and harassed, and town centres are attacked by jihadis.

Across Europe, the EU's own border agency, Frontex, even admits that jihadis have slipped through our porous borders; Merkel opened her doors to one million migrants, mainly young men and some of them repay us by bombing, planning terrorist attacks and attacking our women.

In a devastating report, Frontex (the EU's border control – sic) said the Paris attacks proved jihadists were indeed exploiting the refugee crisis.

The Frontex agency logged a record 1.82 million illegal crossings into the EU in 2015 – six times more than in 2014 and in 2017 we saw half a million – and they are the ones we know about. But it said it had no idea how many illegal migrants there were and, in any case, had no way of tracing their movements inside the EU as there are no border controls due to the open border Schengen system.

Officials also warned a 'staggering' number of European citizens had become jihadists and were taking advantage of lax border controls.

The Paris attacks in November 2015 clearly demonstrated that irregular migratory flows could be used by terrorists to enter the EU,' said the report, Frontex's risk analysis for 2016. 'With no thorough check or penalties in place for those making false declarations, there is a risk that some persons representing a security threat to the EU may be taking advantage of this situation.'

In fact, the number of European jihadists who have joined the ranks of Islamic State has doubled in the last 18 months to around 5,000 today. Two-thirds of them hail from four countries: Belgium, Britain, France and Germany. To add to these woes, about 30% are suspected to have returned to their countries of origin, according to numbers aggregated by the International Centre for Counter-Terrorism.

Our own politicians and some officials not only cover up the atrocities but make excuses for the Muslim migrants' behaviour. They undermine our values and fail to protect our women by suggesting that we cover up, wear more modest clothing, travel with a companion, restrict our intake of alcohol as these acts of 'debauchery' attract unwelcome advances from migrant men. They blame our women for the attacks. Germany and Sweden had to issue notices to the men on how to behave with women. This is outrageous and something the feminazis should be screaming about and demanding action, but they are silent.

Women on the Right uphold our right to act as we wish within the rule of law. Not to do so undermines the struggle of those women who campaigned for votes for women or fought against sexual discrimination and campaigned for equality. We have our rights, the Left's agenda reverses women's rights.

What do the women on the right stand for?

The same as the men. We do not discriminate against men. We share the same policy issues, we just happen to be women.

We believe in the nation state, the sovereignty of our own national parliaments, we believe the EU is undemocratic and is undermining our Western values, we believe open borders, whilst Schengen and uncontrolled immigration is damaging and undermining our own societies and infrastructures.

What we do stand for is choice in the workplace, in the home and in politics. This is not a gender issue.

Women should not made to feel less of a woman if we do not work. The feminizis pushed women into areas that do not necessarily represent their own and their families' interests.

In our universities taxpayers are funding 'gender studies' whose radical feminism presents an extreme negative view of heterosexual relationships and women in the workplace or home. Feminism has been hi-jacked by a narrow elite of radical women who dominate politics and media. Organised for a single purpose – domination – building careers for themselves, creating biases and construct beliefs around their own superiority and views. They want us to believe we are all victims. This poisonous ideology seeks to divide us rather than unite in our differences. They believe there is constant oppression from the patriarchy, men are inherently violent, anyone who contradicts them becomes one of the oppressors and that sexual differences are a cultural imagination, not based on science or biology.

We have marginalized the men. At one end of the spectrum, a walk down any British high street and you will find empowered teenagers pushing prams, mobile phones in hand, with a sperm bank welfare father wandering behind. This poor sperm bank may not be the father of the multiple children that this empowered woman has spawned, encouraged by the State to live on welfare with a home provided by the taxpayers, along with food, nappies and all bills paid. The sperm banks have been reduced to marginalisation with no sense of pride nor responsibility.

In the middle income bracket the women are frazzled because with few male breadwinners they too have to work to pay the mortgage, finance the car and life's other little luxuries. They are mostly responsible for childcare, shopping and household chores because they probably work part-time – and they choose to do so because that is how they divide their responsibilities.

These women – mostly those who work full time – are the most stressed out. They do not network in the bar afterwork because they want to get back to sort out the dirty football bag or do homework with a glass of sauvignon blanc in hand. We are not the weaker sex, just stressed out with the responsibilities.

In the European Parliament they actually debate household division of tasks and decree that men must do more. It is not something you can legislate for, it's something you discuss and manage in the home, as a family. One of the more bizarre pieces of legislation (green crap), they have just made it more difficult for working women - or their cleaners - because they have just cut down the power outage of vacuum cleaners and hairdryers. The mothers get stressed because it takes longer to blow dry their hair whilst at the same time paying more to the cleaner because it takes longer to hoover the home.

In the professional bracket a man may have just become a sperm bank because the feminizis have decided through legislation that we can do it on our own. We can have a child without a man or if we don't like the one that fathered the child/ren then we can always get rid of him. The kids will be put into nurseries provided by the work place (under legislation) or they will go into private childcare (provided under legislation and through the taxpayer), all under the doctrine of gender. As one US writer said, 'We are dads with ovaries'.

We have seen the descriptions of 'mother and father' replaced by 'parent' so that same sex or single parents do not feel stigmatized. 'Married' has disappeared so that we are not judgemental about different lifestyles.

We should ask the questions:

Are women any happier?
Do children brought up in a stable family do better?
What do we want from a stable society?
Do these feminazis represent us?

We have come a long way, what now?

Have we come a long way? Yes, thanks to the campaigning women pre 1980s, not because of the Left's quota systems. It takes a strong woman to become a politician. Putting yourself on the frontline, battling for your causes, being ridiculed, derided and denounced by your opposition in the media and your political opponents.

Your family, friends and colleagues are under scrutiny, particularly in a digital world. Not many women I know want to have this sort of role, and I have tried to persuade other women to stand for election. For us on the Right it is a problem, more so than the liberal left, we come under more attack from the MSM. This allows the gender quotas from the liberal left to thrive.

Gender quotas is not the way forward. The system undermines women, not empower them. In the world of business, women are rejecting any form of quota system, preferring instead to work with the UK government to nudge, educate and encourage employers to train, empower and mentor women to run for top posts. Women want to build their careers based on their own merits, not because they are catapulted into positions based on discriminatory quotas. Norway has forced companies to apply gender quotas, leading to inexperienced women getting into company boards, with overall negative results for the companies involved. That, clearly, helps neither companies nor women.

It used to only be politics that positively discriminated against men and then the feminazis took that campaign into other workplaces. There maybe some very worthy, able and articulate women who have been selected by quotas, but their positions are undermined because they were not selected in a competitive way. The world is competitive, none more so than in politics.

In politics, you have to fight opposite those you would not ordinarily share a platform with. If you cannot fight your corner, you will lose. Therefore, living in a self-imposed safe space silo such as gender quotas is to already be on the losing side.

When they lose the argument they have taken to turning your microphone off, as happened to me twice in the European Parliament in 2018. Mention a topic that they do not wish to raise, then you're cut off. It has happening more frequently with the liberal left MSM, particularly the BBC, where any normal right wing view is constantly interrupted, challenged and then cut off.

I couple of weeks ago I was contacted by a friend of mine who has many insights and contacts within the British Army. A very senior black female officer was concerned that she was being fast-tracked for promotion because she was a black female and was seen as a bit of a poster girl.

She felt she was unprepared for this promotion but was being pressured to accept it. She also fears if she turns down the promotion there will be a nagative mark on her record.

For Europe, direct democracy is the way forward

This is an example of identity politics. In 2018 we saw race being used as a weapon to promote 'black is good', 'white is inferior and racist'. If you are black and female then the world awaits you. Most black women hate this demeaning reverse racism. The world is now digital, the old parties are finding support ebbing away, representative democracy is under threat and I believe direct democracy is the way forward, similar to the Swiss model.

I have long advocated direct democracy. The old parties are frightened of direct democracy believing that their mandate as elected as MPs is sacrosanct. They and the mainstream media would have us believe that the public do not want to be bothered with having to think about complex issues and even that they are uneducated, ill-informed and lazy on major policy areas. Brexit proved them wrong. The rise of Momentum in the UK's socialist party, driven mostly by online support, proved the old guard wrong.

There is a quiet revolution against the old parties. People do not like being branded 'racist', 'xenophobic' and 'uneducated', for wanting their sovereignty back, restricting inward migration or opposing open borders. They see the Left undermining the family, their values and culture.

Social media campaigns and the Brexit debate show that the people are engaged and are capable of making up their own minds when presented with the facts. The mainstream media are key to public engagement, although increasingly are seen as establishment, as we have seen in the Brexit debate but more engagement is increasingly being seen online, particularly amongst women. Trump won, partly because he spoke directly to the people and not through the MSM.

Imagine a world where we could press a button on our computer, text or phone in our views and votes on major issues such as the death penalty, armed conflict, immigration, schooling, taxes, driving offences .... the world would be a better and more dynamic place. And women will lead the way.

European Parliament German socialist, former President Schulz is against direct democracy so it must make sense. He thinks it is just for local government. The trouble is, local government will cease to exist with the federalist EU approach.

As the electorate tilts away from the old politics of Left and Right, perhaps the parties of populism: Austria's FPO,

France's Rassemblement National, Germany's AfD, Finland's Finns, The Netherlands PVV, UK's UKIP/For Britain and now the US's Republicans should re-brand to 'The Populist Party' - to represent 'A person who supports or seeks to appeal to the concerns of ordinary people'?

In the US it is effectively a two party state, perhaps they could do with a bit of DD?

What women want

The trouble is no one asks the ordinary women what they want, it is the politically active that drive the agenda.

We are equal. Yet we are told we are not by a well funded, divisive gender agenda lobby which fans the fuels of resentment whether it is pay, work/life balance, education, health, domestic drudgery, all dressed up in the 'equality debate'.

Why did the Women's Marches in the US, in opposition to Donald Trump becoming president, take place? Women have the same rights as men. Because they didn't vote for Trump, because they hate conservatism, because they've got too much time on their hands and because they are anti-democracy.

I read a bizarre rant by a woman called Dina Leygerman, a writer, apparently, whose shrill piece in The Bigger Picture https://medium.com/bigger-picture/about-your-poem-1f26a7585a6f ticked off all the things that the Women's March were demanding or making reference to.

They demand free everything: healthcare, tampons, abortions, child care, all paid for by the rest of us. In the name of equality, your free tampons equate to men getting free razors too.

She cites a number of areas where the villainous men are still in control and subjugating women. I challenge her here:

1. "Having to carry mace when walking alone at night' – you have the right to bear arms and you're attacked because of wider social problems that the left fail to address.

2. "You still have to prove to a court why you were drunk on the night you were raped ... and have to justify your behavior when a man forces himself on you" – well, ladies, that's justice. There are too many women crying rape as revenge attacks against men and if you are accusing a man of one of the most heinous acts, why shouldn't you have to justify your behavior? After all, he may be going to jail, losing his family, job and reputation.

3. "You have to fight to breastfeed and you still offend others with your breasts" – I get this complaint – babies have to feed and we should not feel ashamed of what we choose to do. If others are offended by your breasts I would suggest that is the work of oppressive religions. And also, a campaign from the left to shut down their view of offensive advertising – underwear, dieting, make-up and nice things like that. You make breasts dirty, not us.

4. "You are still objectified, sexualized and told you are too skinny or too fat, judged on your outfit instead of what's in your head, or what brand of handbag you have" – ladies, how do you think we procreate for the next generation if we do not make ourselves attractive to the opposite sex, it's

nature. I'm glad we tell people they are too skinny and fat – it's not healthy to be either. I like being judged on my outfit, whether I am in the office or out for dinner, we like clothes. As for handbags, the bigger and bolder the better. What would you like to do about the looks obsessed social media teens? Ban social media, ban Vogue, make-up and heels?

5. "You are still being abused by husbands, boyfriends, murdered by partners and being beaten by your soulmate" – er, they're not worth the time effort and heartache, and they're certainly not 'soulmates', how bizarre.

6. "You are still worse of if you are of colour, gay, trans" – I'm not quite sure what 'worse off' means. We are all equal, just some are more equal than others. Some are just weirder.

7. "You, your daughters are not equal and are systematically oppressed" – who makes this stuff up?

8. "Estonia allows parents to take up to three years maternity leave, fully paid" – Estonia, my love, has faced a crisis by its population emptying to find better jobs and futures under the EU's free movement of people. Drastic times, drastic measures. It's about re-populating, not social progress.

9. "Singapore's women feel safe" – ahem, Singapore has the death penalty, I am sure you would like it repealed in the States?

She goes on, and on and on ….

She thinks we believe feminists are emotional, irrational and unreasonable. No, we think you are feminazis, taking up causes that the ordinary woman working in WalMart or Wall Street doesn't think are important.

Apparently, we want to feel empowered and don't want to feel we are oppressed but she is offering to walk for me and our daughters because one day we will be equal.

We have won our rights and we thank the sisters that pioneered them in the last century. Your type of festering feminazi hate is corrosive, nasty and not what women want.

The Feminists, formerly considered radicals, now subversives, stand up for ordinary women.

Linda Bellos, a hard line feminist of the left is barred from one of our world class universities, Cambridge.

After suggesting she would be "publically questioning some of the trans politics ... which seems to assert the power of those who were previously designated male to tell lesbians, and especially lesbian feminists, what to say and think". Brilliant stuff. And then ...

Ailish Maroof, the co-president of the society, which describes itself as a "gender and feminism" group, replied: "I'm sorry but we've decided not to host you. I too believe in freedom of expression, however Peterhouse is as much a home as it is a college. The welfare of our students in this instance has to come first."

In response, our girl Bellos, banging the drum for all of us said, "I'm not being told by someone who a few months ago was a man what I as a woman can or cannot do". Well done that woman. https://www.thetimes.co.uk/article/linda-bellos-barred-in-cambridge-university-row-0pbdq5sm9?shareToken=3fc6ee763138dff14536abcafc64cf5c

However, before we start applauding, Cambridge gels are still getting their knickers in a twist. An all-female college will now accept anyone who identifies as female, as "gender is not binary".

Cambridge's Murray Edwards College has now decided that students who think they are women will be eligible for a place.

The college that was founded to address gender imbalance is now abandoning that mission. If this college doesn't believe that gender is binary and they shouldn't be a single sex college. I'd love to be a fly on the wall in the resident halls when the men identifying as women start waving their willies in the bathrooms under the showers. And to think we fund these institutions. If they want to go down this bonkers route then perhaps they should consider self funding, raising cash like US colleges and then they can be totally autonomous as well as androdynous. (No platforming is an unchecked infectious disease in our universities).

There's no sisterhood in politics, the sex and sleaze of European politics

I've detailed the political antics of the European Parliament so now let's talk about sex.

Recently some women in Parliament leaked to the media certain sexual harassment claims against men. I'm sure they were telling the truth about their male bosses, but there is another side to the story.

When I entered the European Parliament in 2014 I was struck by the beautiful, intelligent, multi lingual young people, all highly paid, who worked for MEPs. High heels, short skirts, plunging necklines, with first class degrees and languages.

I had heard of the affairs, young women who were ambitious, some for their careers, but others wondering who they could take to bed, to be a concubine for a politician with power, or to usurp the long standing wife.

From the left and right, they targeted the men. Did it happen the other way around? Yes, but less so. The EU is a hotbed of sex, a free for all. I saw what happened during and after hours.

Imagine 751 successful, well paid, influential politicians. All away from home for at least four days a week. A good salary, chauffeurs with limos, hotels, apartments, expense accounts, foreign trips with business class air fares and hotels, mixing with foreign diplomats and foreign governments, all under the guise of a 'Mission' - an official trip for the EU committees.

The young women who target the male MEPs flagrantly encouraging them to think with other parts of their anatomy than their brains. Inevitably some of them fall into the honey trap of thinking these young, pretty, intelligent women find them attractive for their looks or erudition. Maybe one or two do but most are after a lifestyle of hotels, booze, limos and foreign trips.

Or they are simply using these men are a stepping stone – often simply a rung on the ladder of the political ladder in their own country. They can actually be predatory - roaming the corridors of power in Brussels and the bars, flaunting their CV's with glossily taken photographs. They can resemble sirens on the sea luring the EU hapless sailors, drunk onpower, influence and often alcohol too, to the rocks of their ambition.

Equally, there are male MEPs who – sometimes aggressively, sometimes in more oleaginous ways - set out to lure and target young women, craving the male status symbol of a pretty young thing in . They scour hundreds of CVs for the cuties, overlooking the gaps in their education and language skills when the looks compensate. At home these men are often seen as mediocre creatures, sent out to the EU as out of sight, out of mind. They are important in the EU and yet they abuse their status. They use the girls for sex, to organise their private lives and their party status.

The MEPs sleeping with each other. Power likes power. I've seen bitter enemies in the debating chamber text each other in committee and delegation meetings, giving covert looks, sexting and leaving the debates to have sex in the nearest toilet. They fight bitterly with their political allies to get onto foreign trips so they can be away with their lovers. They can almost live together because no one is watching. I know a prominent German MEP who sleeps with a bitter rival. She sleeps with interns, senior staffers and MEPs. She goes back to her home country at the weekend to be with her husband and children. He reports back to Mutti Merkel.

Female MEPs are only slightly better than the men. They're predators too. Employing good looking younger male 'advisors' who fawn over the women and who will do what it takes to get to that next step up on the career ladder.

The sex business does a good trade in Brussels. Like most cities there are prostitutes plying their trade for every palate and wallet. While the left and the sisterhood talk about the abuse and victimhood of prostitutes and how they should be shut down (probably to be enrolled in a wimmins' collective) some of us see them as business women. Some are tied to drug dealing pimps (and that is another issue entirely), but those that take the euro from MEPs know exactly what they are doing.

Aside from the sexual exploitation, I have witnessed very senior political figures from Germany openly verbally abusing and humiliating their staff, mainly young women. They have screamed at their supposed ineptitude in public corridors but their only rebuke is 'did you hear old fatty x screaming at another young staff member?' It's almost normal behaviour in the warped behaviour patterns which infect this darker and unseen side of Brussels.

The activities of Brussels thriving and substantial gay community also merit scrutiny on this score. Just as with their heterosexual counterparts, many of them have no qualms about cross party cooperation of various descriptions when it comes to career advancement. Some target their MEPs to take on their bright young thing lovers. Some gay MPs, understandably, give priority to hiring fellow gays. This gives the opportunity for sexual favours to play their part in career advancement in Brussels.

By the same token, some lesbians on the alt Left give only employ other lesbians, homosexuals or trans. It might be a point for discussion were straight MEPs and Brussels aides to employ similarly narrow recruitment criteria but in this as in so many things, this is the Brussels world as it is, not as it should be.

I was once told by a senior Labour MEP that I was a 'stupid fucking woman" because I called into question the damaging legislation imposed upon UK business by Brussels. Overheard, he subsequently denied it, in writing despite knowing that I had witnesses. Imagine, I asked him, if one of my male colleagues from the Right said that about one of your women? But because I am from the Right different rules apply. They can sometimes seem dangerously close to that antediluvian justification for sexual abuse and worse of "well, she was asking for it….."

On another occasion, I was dangerously chased by a British journalist working for a Brussels media outlet. We had agreed to an interview a few months before when he arrived late and drunk, swilling a glass of red wine. It was 10 in the morning. When I raised an eyebrow and asked whether this was acceptable at this hour he replied: "You're UKIP, I would have thought it's normal for you." I took up the matter with his editor but my complaint was dismissed out of hand.

A few months later the same journalist drunkenly chased me along a slippery wooden gangway in Strasbourg, with a heavy TV camera on his shoulder and a plate glass wall on my other side. In heels, I slid along the slippery floor trying to get away from him, aware that should this hefty drunken man slip then I would be in some measure of danger. I was lucky to escape his reach.

Yet when I raised this in a debate about violence against women with high representative Mrs Moghereni from the unelected Commission in attendance, there was silence across the chamber. It's OK for them to debate violence in the home, violence against vulnerable women and migrant women. But when it comes to defending the women on the Right, the silence was deafening. It said a lot about what level is tolerated from whom towards whom.

I was also a victim of sex on tap. My former assistant was let loose in the corridors of sex and power. Unleashed from her former job and leaving her husband behind, this mid 50's woman acted like an alley cat with an elected male colleague. She stayed in his hotel rooms, openly sat in bars and restaurants a deux, creeping back to my hotel room she shared with me or to the office just before dawn. Unfortunately for me (and subsequently for her) she didn't keep a watch on emailed instructions about an event. She has now got a criminal record and I sit as an independent MEP.

There are always consequences for people's actions.

Again, the Neanderthal element of "well, dressed in views like that, she's asking for it". That such a revolting level of abuse can be tolerated simply because of views held is a damning indictment of our new moral code of victimhood. Imagine, just for a moment, that such behaviour were inflicted women of the Left. The screams about women's rights, human rights and male oppression would be heard from Brussels to London and beyond!

Sexual harassment has long been rife in Brussels and it is time that the lid was lifted on it. But in doing so, we should remember that it is not simply male on female. And that there is an unspoken pact that some deserve abuse and aggression for the views they hold. It is a scandal on so many levels. Last year, they finally got to grips with how to deal with sexual harrassment and bullying in the workplace. However, the judge, jury and executioner is a small MEP committee that decides on the evidence presented that you are guilty or not. If you are found guilty they will strip you of your mandate and inform the media. I asked why the file isn't sent to the MEP's home country policeforce first before his/her life is destroyed? This was met with increduality. At least they can get Viagra on the EU's health scheme.

Chapter 10

My friend the Trans Woman

From man to woman, – the story of a friend of mine, who has transgendered and now has a happy relationship with a man.

As I explained in Chapter 6, there are a small number of people who genuinely have gender dysphoria. This is one of them.

Transgender the Experience By Deborah Williams

I write this years' on after transition as both a reflective on my experiences and a commentary on the current state of the world we live in. I remain anonymous since in this sad world there are those that may disagree with my position who will attempt to "dox" me to cause trouble in my professional work, particularly those on the left who wish to endlessly divide the world into ever smaller "victim" groups that can be mobilised to support their redistributive agenda.

The first fact I would point out is that having transgendered, I am not "transgender" or part of the "trans" community. I did not go through this to become some sort of freak to be photographed for the more excitable parts of the media, I was diagnosed with a disorder as described, medically, by Dr. Harry Benjamin in 1966. The International Classification of Diseases 10_{th} edition (ref) describes is as one of five recognised "Gender Identity Disorders" (GID) (Capetillo-Ventura, Jalil-Pérez, & Motilla-Negrete, 2015, p. 54) with a clear ethology mentioning the linkage with brain formation and hormone exposure in mid to late stage pregnancy(ibid, p54-5), the end point of which is transition, as far as physically possible, to the opposite sex and taking the social responsibilities, disadvantages and benefits thereon.

The story of Transition

I suppose that it would be easy to say I felt like a girl from an early part of my life. This would be disingenuous at best. being something of a sickly child I did not like sport much, but played as any other child; climbing trees, getting filthy and as life was in the countryside in the middle of the last century doing a lot of hiking and camping with other children on our own. Nowadays the safety lobby would be horrified but this was a typical life of a child growing up in the English countryside. I was dimly aware that I was uncomfortable about growing up, but my maturity was late and I was grateful not to have to confront the whole process. My thoughts were that I just hoped that by some miracle of development I would develop the "other way"; when I did not I learned meditation to suppress and avoid the whole issue. This was not without consequence, but people who knew me just assumed I was either a closeted gay or not interested at all.

As I grew to adulthood, the treatment of, sometimes former professional, transgendered women was truly shocking. It used to be said that the News of the World, a paper that has subsequently collapsed, used to publish the "tranny of the month"; some poor unfortunate that had been outed by the media and had their photograph slated all over the centre pages of that rag. Since this generally destroyed what was already a fragile life, it was a terrible warning for all those who might follow down a similar path; social pariah-hood, rejection by family and friends and destruction of the career. Very few people made transition in that time without consequence and I had no desire to experience a similar fate.

I suppose a warning to me was that by burying myself in work, often doing an 80 hour week, I was also descending into bad health, making myself socially isolated, drinking too much and eating badly at the same time. I later discovered that this is expressed as a *"clinically significant distress or impairment in social, occupational or other important areas of functioning"* (Lawrence, 2008, p. 426) is one of the common expressions of gender dysphoria and sought treatment.

One of the problems with the British NHS is that it has always been rationed and stressed. As a small part of a not well funded treatment area, Britain offered one centre for the treatment of gender identity issues at the Charing Cross Hospital in London (actually in Hammersmith, West London). As can be imagined this had a waiting list to shame all other waiting lists. The general press treated it badly suggesting that every other treatment took priority over *"cosmetic surgery"* (anecdotal). Therefore I had 8 months kicking around before I could see a psychiatrist. In this time, as I had feared from all my expectations from my youth, I lost my job and home end ended up living with friends in London. Being a grand capital city, I soon found the transgender and gay community living there. The lesbian community generally hated male to female transgendered people but more on that later.

Amongst the clubs, I found them to be pretty open and friendly, learning more about others with a similar condition. Although living was hard, I was periodically able to go to the clubs and get to know the different tribes in the LGBT "community".

Up to this point I had no idea how the different groups in the LGBT world would treat me. Most surprising, I suppose, were the "bears"; larger men, who liked other larger me, preferably hairy. They were always the most generous and welcoming of all the people I met, and I still keep in touch with many of them. Worst were the "Twinks"; self-absorbed types who would be uncomfortable unless someone is admiring them, body obsessed and rather narcissistic. I suppose the oddest were the people in the fetish clubs who liked some of the outfits that I, and others on my path, would come up with and sometimes would say "respect to the radical body modification" as one particularly pierced individual said.

The final group was the Drag scene who had their own clubs, from the infamous "Ron Storm's Tea Dance" that started in the 1960's, to the "Way Out Club" still running in London this day. It had plusses and minuses. The drag queens themselves were usually gay men who dressed up in a fantastic artifice of womanhood, fun, but an exaggerated mockery. I am told anecdotally that the origins of this were in the 1800's music halls where men dressed as exaggerated women as comedy, although the real origins may be possibly earlier in theatre where women were banned from the stage and thus men would play their part. I still love the mix of music, comedy and risqué entertainment that the drag artists come up with.

Others in this group were men who had bisexual fantasies that could only be let out when they were "dragged up". The spectrum of this scene went from those who looked similar to the Drag Queens, looking to cavort with others to those who dressed in some illusion of a 1960's librarian; twin set and pearls. All had their view of what a cross dresser should look like from the overtly fetishist club look, sported in modern pop videos, to that weirdly conservative look that was the look of those in the "Beaumont Society". The dark side of this part of the London scene was that once the most overtly gay are excluded, there was something of a social order where people were encouraged to "go full transition", many of these going on into prostitution, particularly amongst those who wanted "chicks with dicks"; some using the money earned for surgery (McClear, 2011, p. 164), others happy to remain somewhere in-between getting sexual kicks whilst outwardly appearing to be a woman. Since getting the hormones required medical prescriptions, those who had already gone down this path would coach newcomers in what to say to psychiatrists to get the results they wanted; useful for the girls on the game, but in this environment mistakes were bound to happen as in the case of Russel Reid, a psychiatrist in London (Batty, 2007) and as highlighted more recently (Shute, 2017).

So I transitioned socially, taking the precaution to move from one place as a male to a new place as outwardly female, presenting myself as a jeans and t shirt chic young woman. Fortunately I had slight build and little body or facial hair, so as long as I kept myself to myself no one challenged me; I kept myself in a little bubble of a world where I had some friends around me and could survive. At some point the welfare system decided that they would send me on courses to get back to work. I had worked on the assumption, based on the treatment meted on people by the press in my youth, that there was no chance of my getting a meaningful job. Certainly not a professional job or one where I would not suffer threats to my person. I was lucky enough to be under the tutelage of an inspiring ex recruitment consultant who guided me towards the emerging IT world, one which was a bit more relaxed about everything and where I could hide amongst the armies of temps that served in London. I got a short term job shortly after, knowing that that if I was "outed" then I could move on pretty swiftly; most of these positions requiring at most one weeks' notice to move on. More importantly I had money.

One of the issues I had with the public health system was both that the appointments were astoundingly infrequent and that they would get cancelled at short notice. A torture that they invented was the group therapy session. Whilst group therapy can have benefits; see the APA guidelines (Science to Service Task Force, 2007) twenty or so people sitting in a circle being asked one by one "how do you feel" does not strike me as being entirely in line with best practice, even at that time.

The only benefit of this circus was in meeting one or two other people in work who introduced me to clinicians in private practice. After one especially excruciating session, and my therapist yet again cancelling an appointment at zero days' notice, I told them I was not returning and would go to a private consultant. To be fair they did take it gracefully, I guess I was one person off their backlog of cases. The private clinicians quickly referred me to a surgeon and were somewhat confused by the time it had taken to get to that point. Because of the challenge of taking 6 weeks out of my career by this point, it was another two years before I actually got to have the surgery.

I suppose after this my life became rather boring. Work, Vacations, Relationships; a rather normal life. After many years just plodding on, more work, better vacations, just living quietly and with a very un-public life but I have been relatively successful. The process turned me from an unhappy young man to a successful and relatively content older woman; chalk up a success.

The most disturbing part of my journey really has been the attitude of the left. Aside from the openly hostile attitude of many of them, the tendency to bring people onto television as part of some sort of freak show illustrates the gutter that many outlets have sunk to. When I consider the attitudes of right and left, it is telling that the first transgendered national representative from the UK was elected on a UKIP ticket. I do look forward to the time when it does not matter but keep in mind the words of my psychiatrist that the first test of being truly transgender is that the patient wishes to transition and live presenting, and being accepted in, the target gender role.

What is Transgenderism

Although this essay is biographical, I wanted to touch on the medical background. The term in internationally accepted medical taxonomy is part of a group of medical disorders in adults accepted as part of the International Statistical Classification of Diseases and Related Health Problems (Lawrence, 2008, p. 428) (Capetillo-Ventura, Jalil-Pérez, & Motilla-Negrete, 2015, p. 54) with can have origins in early development (Mah, Chan, & Yang, 2017) this is extremely rare and there is really insufficient epidemiological evidence to show that there is a *"significant impact on population, rather transgenderism has a very broad and variable spectrum in different individuals in terms of perception of cross-gender identity"* (Feldberg, 2017, p. 63). The instance of transgenderism is low studies suggesting that the prevalence is roughly one in thirty thousand men and one in one hundred thousand women (Capetillo-Ventura, Jalil-Pérez, & Motilla-Negrete,

2015, p. 54). With "*the important clinical principle of 'Do No Harm*" (Coleman, 2017, p. 71) there is now clear evidence that reassignment does reduces the risk of attempted suicide (ibid.), which in some studies has been shown to be as high as 55% in male to female transgender patients and 46% in female to male (Lawrence, 2008, p. 438). However, standards of care and "gatekeeping" for people who present themselves for treatment can be variable as is perhaps indicated by an increase in "re-reassignment" surgery (Shute, 2017). As observed above from anecdotal evidence there is social pressure on people with non-transgender dysphoria to transition, coaching from colleagues in the social grouping that enable them to fool healthcare professionals in the first instance. This is underlined by Lawrence who notes that "*clients sometimes deliberately or unintentionally give distorted accounts of their histories or feelings*" (Lawrence, 2008, p. 440) It is telling "*that as many as 50% of persons who undergo evaluation*"…"*leave treatment*"(ibid p,435). It should be noted that clinicians also have to work through other "Co Morbid" factors that include schizophrenia, substance abuse and self-harm (Lawrence, 2008, pp. 436-7).

My final point is on the treatment of young adults and even children. The most worrying aspects are highlighted in recent work on the subject where concerns over the ability of a young adult to make such decisions in the pre-adolescent stages are highlighted such as the known gender fluidity at this stage, the social impact, the development of sexual behaviour resulting from hormone suppression and future medical issues (Giovanardi, 2017, p. 154). Further there is a lack of epidemiological evidence on the long term effects of this treatment, underlined by Shute's article (op cit.). More work is clearly needed to determine whether such treatment should be widely available.

Conclusion

I would stress that I am not a medical professional, I am researching in the light of political questions being asked about the underlying validity and generosity of availability of transgender surgery, commenting on erudite professionals writings in as neutral a position as possible, given I am myself transgendered.

As I sum up, it is clear that in some cases, reassignment surgery is the best outcome for a person who is distressed due to gender dysphoria. For myself I have lived, worked and prospered as a transgendered person achieving both academic and professional success in my chosen social role. The apparent rise in post-operative regression and suicide does give rise to question the reliability of treatment given to people seeking help, but the underlying validity of treatment is well researched and now has good epidemiological evidence to show that it is the best treatment in some cases for people with severe gender dysphoria.

Do I have regrets, perhaps, as in quieter moments I wonder what life might have been, but I remind myself of my feelings of confusion and a need to seek help as I walked through a rainy Shepherds Bush Market to catch the overland tube to the Charing Cross Hospital, then the only public hospital providing service for gender dysphoria in the UK.

And Finally on Toilets…

The people who did not and still in many case do not show any sympathy or care for transgendered women are the hard feminist movement. Worst of these are the "TERFS" who at various times have suggested that transgendered people should simply be locked up, away from the rest of the community. If a phobia is described as an irrational fear of something, the fear of transgendered people merely because of their transgendered nature is genuinely irrational. All groups of people are a mixed bag, you get the good with the bad, and the crazy with the inspirational, there will be genuinely manipulative and destructive people in the group that is transgendered, just as any other group.

The issue seems to be derived from the concept of fundamental violence in men which is exacerbated by the blurring of the lines between the spectrum of people who cross dress to those who live as women but retain their male physical aspects, and finally those who transition. They make the assumption that *"men are impulsive and predatory"... "Spreading faeces around the toilet in a way that women do not"* (Jeffreys, 2014, p. 43) the latter which seems a little unfair. Looking at the observed behaviour of people in the cross dressing world, I can understand the threat involved: it is telling that gay and cross dressing pubs and clubs either install defensive measures to stop substance abuse and sexual behaviour in toilets, even having security guards in women's toilets in some cases. As mentioned above there is a considerable difference in the behaviour between transgender people and the wide range of cross dressers and those who have hormone treatment to enhance their sexual experience. The problem is that lumping post-operative transgendered people in with people who cross dress for fun, or sexual reasons, muddies the water in a way that makes any debate nonsensical and creates the febrile environment where naturally born women are assaulted for entering a women's toilet simply because they appear not to conform to a stereotype.

What is also shown here is that the blurring of lines between transsexual people and transvestites. A transsexual women lives in the social role with all the problems, challenges and threats that one born does, and were the TERFs to be honest, then they would recognise that.

Chapter 11

My friend, Trannie

My friend, Trannie, is a six foot tall, hunky man who, in his teens and early twenties says he had no real clue about who he was, he identified as straight and now in his 50s he's gay.

He says it was his choice and was pleased at not being forced to decide his gender.

Trannie, tells his story:

I grew up in a matriarchy, the youngest child. I loved my older sisters and was enraptured by all things feminine, and I loved playing with Barbie dolls. I knew that I was a boy and part of me regretted that I wouldn't grow up to have lush lips, wide hips and long flowing locks. If someone had asked me "would you like to be a girl", and if they could have waved a magic wand, then my answer would have been "YES!" with no hesitation. The notions of surgery and sexual reassignment and the suppression of puberty weren't available in the industrial days of my youth, and so I ventured into an androgynous teenage wilderness and came out the other side as a man who dresses as a woman on a lot of occasions.

I'm glad that surgery wasn't an option in my youth. I stand at almost 6 feet tall, with broad shoulders, a blokish face, and manly hands. It wouldn't have been enough to give me daily doses of estrogen or a nose job and a brow-shaving; no, I would have needed my whole skeleton reformed in order to approach the semblance of a female. Walking around the streets dressed as a woman today invites all sorts of responses from people. People tend to have no filter when they see me dressed up. I am met with every emotion from love through anger and ridicule and on to outright rage. And this is fine because I can go home and take it all off, and then I can go about my business looking like a man without having to be trapped in the simulacrum of an unconvincing female's body. How detrimental to my mental health that would be. I've chosen to make peace with the hand I have been dealt in life instead. I prefer being dressed as a female, I feel beautiful, empowered and free. It's a creative act of expression for me, and it's akin to playing God on one level. I create this glorious creature from scratch. I breathe life into her and give her shape and form. I strap on my breasts, paint my face into a character unrecognizable from my boy self, and I make and design my own clothing so that I can most truly and uniquely be the external representation of how I feel myself to be inside.

It's perplexing to me, today, to hear people say that they feel like a woman trapped inside a man's body. This is unquantifiable nonsense. I'm a male and I couldn't tell anyone what it feels like to feel like a man. I recognise the differences between the sexes (penis, denser muscle mass, greater physical strength, thicker and tougher skin, peeing standing up, etc.) but there is no one feeling or attribute that I have which makes me feel like a man. I feel like a human being and I'm sure I share all of my feelings, to greater or lesser degrees, with all other human beings, male and female alike. I feel hunger, cold, the need for touch, the need for creative satisfaction, love and friendship, etc., all universal feelings that all humans share. And not one of them specific to being a man or a woman. These men who feel that they are women trapped in men's bodies, to my mind, are simply people with an attraction to or an admiration for a particular type of woman and they feel what they imagine she must feel like as she's going about her busty, high-heeled business. They have a false notion that they're buying into. No man who feels like a woman ever feels menopausal or pre-menstrual – none of them ever appear in public as though they've just finished doing the dishes, or have just dropped the kids off at school. All of it utter nonsense, all of it nothing more than sexual fetishism for the most part.

You'll find the majority of trannies keep their penises and opt for getting the biggest pair of breasts available. Real women don't have penises, so why do these trannies keep theirs if they feel like women? Their penises are their money-makers. Prostitution is rife in the tranny world, and it's not because society is excluding them, or being unkind and unforgiving to them. These dudes with boobs (chicks don't have dicks) and the men who enjoy having sex with them (trannychasers) are essentially just men in wigs who are negotiating a sex act. They are as horny as you'd expect any man to be, and they do not mind doing sex work for a living, they do not mind it one bit. They travel the country doing it because it's big business and there's a lot of money to be made from it, easy money.

If you can afford it, or if you live in a country where sexual reassignment surgery is part of the national health scheme, then you can cut and chop and sculpt your body until your little heart is content. But you still need to live with the emotional and psychological impact of your actions and the fact that your blood reading will say you're a man, even though you're dressed as a woman, and vice versa. Naked, the scarring on your body from having your breasts removed or inserted will be a daily reminder that you're not a genetic male or female, coupled with all of those pills you're swallowing. It's a sign of a deeper societal madness that we are indulging trans people in their delusions, and particularly worrying that we are now indulging children in theirs (as a result of being exposed to information that is not age-appropriate – 98% of 'confused' boys allowed to go through puberty without hormone therapy turn out to be perfectly happy with their birth gender).

All of this nonsense is being pushed by pharmaceutical companies (it's a big money business) and the LGBT (get my T out of your LGB because being T has nothing to do with sexuality – a lot of men who dress up are heterosexual and married and wouldn't touch another man). The political gay lobby are using the tranny issue as a tool to beat people over the head with. You have 'body positive' (fat) dykes (lesbians) with moustaches out on the streets screaming now that 'tranny' is a bad word. Tranny is not a bad word. Every tranny I know uses the word tranny in relation to themselves and their friends. A few prefer t-girl, but those are the more delusional ones. In London, prior to being closed for refurbishment, we had a nightclub called the Trannyshack, and every year they held competitions looking for the next big tranny superstar (a weekly talent contest with rounds of elimination until finally we came down to the best couple of acts). And this club also held yearly Christmas tranny-balls, and the men (admirers) who came to the clubs looking to hook up with the 'gals' are called trannychasers. Tranny is not a bad word, it's an umbrella term that includes cross-dressers, transvestites, dudes with boobs, sexual fetishists, hairy pantie wearers (the older and more unconvincing of the gals, and usually with no makeup skills or taste in clothing), and all other sort of androgyne. The trannyshack nightclub in San Fransisco, of all places, had to change its name because of the bullying LGBT. RuPaul had to stop saying his catch-phrase, "Hooo, gurrlll, you have a she-mail" (a notification for one of the contestants by a viewer such as a vote or comment). RuPaul paved the way for drag queens and cross-dressers, and even still the political body of the LGBT turned on him, claiming that his catch-phrase had a disturbing impact on men who identify as women. They claimed that it belittled them, and caused emotional distress, to which I would tell them to 'man up'.

I prefer being called a tranny because that is who and what I am. The only people I would call 'trans' are those men and women who have fully committed to their sexual reassignment, and who have had their penises removed as well as their wombs. If you're doing it by half-measures, you're a tranny. It's disrespectful to trans people to call a dude with boobs anything but a tranny (since we're all being forced to be PC these days with our speech). You'll also find that these trans men and women who have undergone surgery to the fullest extent aren't part of the tranny scene. They're usually living quiet lives in the suburbs, getting on with their lives and careers, and they're not involved in the sex circuit that is so prevalent and common among trannies. But just as with race (the thing that gives the left the biggest and hardest erection today – it's their viagra), trannies are now, without our permission, being used by a body that certainly does not represent myself nor any of the people I know. The left have taken it upon themselves to latch onto what they perceive to be an aggrieved minority group in order to weaponize themselves and they are using trannies as their bullets and bombs.

The biggest victims in all of this are women. Women are losing their rights and their identity in the face of the rise of this very small percentage of men who allegedly have a female trapped inside their bodies (studies range between 0.3 to 0.5% of the population). Women are having to share their personal spaces with men, such as changing rooms and communal showers. Women are having to compete in sports against men (contact sports in some instances, like cage-fighting, in which someone could easily be killed). Women are having to share jail cells with men who identify as female. Women are now "pregnant people", not pregnant women, because to say that only women can become pregnant is to remind the man on hormones that he'll never give birth. I see pictures of women on hormones, covered in chest hair, who identify as men and yet they choose to keep their wombs and they choose to give birth, coz you know nothing makes you feel more manly than lactating does. And pictured on the front of the newspaper, the headline ecstatically yells FIRST MAN IN THE UK TO GIVE BIRTH. The title is false – it should read 'female on hormones in UK gives birth'. It's boring. Yawn. Give me real news. The accompanying picture is sickening. Females tend to look more realistic when they transition. The hormones cause them to have male-pattern baldness and their bodies become covered with hair. And there you have a newborn suckling on a hairy teat. It's child abuse. A hair could get lodged in the baby's throat. Or another couple of parents who both transitioned; dad became mum, and mum became dad. It's narcissistic and self-indulgent. And this madness extends into the military and into the high school, where all that's needed to enter female spaces is to say that you identify as a woman. Beauty houses are selling female beauty products while using a tranny as the face of the beauty cream. Male skin is different to female skin, so this is false advertising mixed with a lot of airbrushing. How can you use male skin to show how wonderfully a female beauty cream works on female flesh?

Do-gooders and bullies are attempting to reshape reality, and we are seeing words changing their meanings, in order to accommodate trans people. By all means, live your life, go about your business unharmed. Express yourself and find comfort dressing and living however you please without being met with restrictions or violence, but do not enforce your delusions onto me and do not expect to change the way I see the world. My right to dress as a woman does not carry with it the right to bully other people's language. Misgender me all you please, because you won't be misgendering me – I am a man in a dress, so by all means call me 'Sir', it won't be a crime, it will be the truth and it will be your reality. New York has laws in place where people are being heavily fined if they misgender someone. This is more madness. If I see a man in a dress, he's getting called 'he'. If I see a very convincing man in a dress who is living full-time as a woman and he really is having me question my eyesight because I'm not 100% sure if I'm looking at a male or female, then kudos to you and I'll call you 'she'. But I'll call you what I call you on my terms, and based on what my eyes and brain are registering. I won't be bullied into using your words to pander to your delusions about yourself, and I won't bully you into changing the way you view me. I don't think society cares about, or is bothered by, trans people to the extent that we're being told we do. The left are blowing it out of all proportion and doing trannies an injustice in the meantime. It's the bullying that people object to, not the dress.

Rupert Everett, actor, warns against hormone therapy for kids who question gender: "I really wanted to be a girl. Thank God the world of now wasn't then, because I'd be on hormones and I'd be a woman. After I was 15 I never wanted to be a woman again."

Chapter 12

Introduction to John, gay and happy, not transgender

I came across John, not his real name, a year ago. He is on the Right of politics and a very talented young man, as is his partner. They will be household names one day.

He had been led down the path of transgenderism and was very bitter against the people that had treated him.

He confided to me that he now felt embarrassed by his body and that he had approached various doctors to have a full reversal via surgery of the femalisation of his body. Despite stopping the hormones and mostly reversing the effects, he still didn't look or feel fully male. He has been refused.

And we are going to see many more Johns.

I can remember with rather surprising clarity the three hours I spent with a psychologist in a rather blunt but fairly named 'psychosexual problems' clinic. It was 2011 and I had been referred by an NHS GP (several in fact) to the clinic to talk about transgenderism. The waiting list had been long, and I had become evermore cemented in my transition as I waited almost a year for my referral to bear fruit. By the time the three hour interview rolled around I was certain of two things; I was transgender and this was interview was about box ticking. What followed was perhaps the most arduous box-ticking I have been through before or since. For three hours I was drilled on my childhood, my relationship with my parents, my school years, my fears and aspirations, my experience of puberty, my sex life, my libido, sexual positions, fetishes, experiences, partners, relationships and so on. What had been sold to me as an introductory meeting to 'get to know the doctor' quickly became a roaring, delving, no-holds-barred, fight-for-your-life deconstruction of my entire life right up until that very day. And then, almost as quickly as it had begun it was over. I was certifiably transgender. I got my little scrawl of red ink on some doctor's note or another and just like that I was 'referred', happily added to another waiting list, this time for the Charing Cross (its not in Charing Cross) Gender Identity Clinic where I would ultimately be prescribed hormones without a minute's more counseling than I had just had. From then on all that stood between me and Hormone Replacement Therapy was time.

It may sound odd but until that moment I had never really considered the implications of my upbringing or sexuality on my gender identity. I'd had a fairly normal childhood, being raised in an affluent white upper middle class British family and having been a friend to everyone in an all boys Grammar school. My parents raised me as a boy and had no reason or inclination to raise me any other way. I had known I was homosexual from my early teens (I try to avoid using the terms homosexual and gay interchangeably as in 2018 I feel they represented vastly different things), but even that I feel played little part in my later gender confusion. It wasn't until much later I began to accumulate a more interesting social group, counting transgender people, drag queens and club kids among my closest friends.

Over time I fell in with a crowd of interesting, unique people who ultimately existed outside the realms of heterosexual culture. I came up through the club scene where pulling off outlandish 'looks' and performing in drag bars were a way to earn your stripes and climb to the top of the social strata, having paid your dues to more seasoned queens of course. Over time this became my normality and my friends became my second family. Transgenderism became normal to me and everyone was 'she', something that just made life easier in drag culture though its unconscious impact would become clear later on. At some point the wigs and the heels and the makeup ceased to be a preserve of nighttime shenanigans and it just became who I was. My drag name became the name everyone knew my by and ultimately the name my family would call me. Looking back I think it fortunate I didn't pick some ridiculous sexual pun to go by, instead opting for a simple Issy, which would later become Isabelle. There is strength in numbers and when you dress up and party for attention, doing it in the daytime feels utterly normal as long as you have a few good friends doing it too.

So by the time I got my referral to the Gender Clinic and had my first session with an endocrinologist (blood doctor) I had been living full time as a female for two years. I was enrolled in university, had a steady job and a thriving social life. Going in to my first appointment I was untouchable. I was seasoned compared to the nervous, poorly dressed patients around me - even finding myself annoyed at their sloppily applied makeup and fairly masculine take on how women were supposed to dress (I've never seen so many studded work boots and fishnets in my life). On top of that I was brave . That's what everyone told me. I never experienced transphobia or violence. Sure there was the odd insensitive question or poorly worded introduction, but they were always made with the genuine intention to understand - and when they did people were in of this brave, innocent, transgressive saint that trans people are these days. So I was straight through. A few blood tests, a few more boxes to tick - "Do you have a job?" "Are you in a relationship", that sort of thing. The way Gender Clinics work is you have an appointment every six months (the time between appointments being mostly down to the sheer volume of patients at each clinic - some are even in the thousands at any one time), and you have every appointment twice. You have two consultants and you'll alternate which one you see, the idea being that they can cross reference notes (make sure you still have a job) and move you along to the next step provided everything fits.

So I went to my appointments, did the time, talked about how having a relationship and studying at universirty meant I was normal and functioning and that was it. In just over a year I was on hormones. Oestrogen to feminise the body and anti-androgens (a rather nasty slow-release capsule injected in the tummy every three months) to block testosterone production. I never had an appreciation for the importance of hormones until I screwed around with them. These things really do turn you into a woman, sort of. I was emotional, hysterical, lost interest in action movies, my libido went down, the amount of alcohol it took to get me drunk was cut in half, I was suddenly interested in cuddling after sex and then there were the physical changes. I developed breasts, my skin softened and became more sheer, fat moved around my body and my waist got smaller while my hips and buttocks got a lot bigger. It wasn't until I stopped hormones and finally reverted to my natural state that I realised how big the difference had been.

Ultimately I began to question the need to change myself. The doctors had the clinic had openly said it was something in the brain, in the mind itself. I remember so clearly my first day at Charing Cross, hearing the words "we just don't know enough about the brain to do anything so we have to change the body to match". It should have sent alarm bells ringing then. This is all too new I should have thought, we don't know enough about how or why this happens my rational self would have concluded. Eventually I did and I began to think that if nobody gave me my body then it couldn't be wrong, and if it isn't wrong then why should I change it. Sure I still had a lot of the feelings, the hard to describe sense that the way I had come to look and be was just me . But surely that was something I should be discovering for myself, not corroborating with medication while I waited for life changing and irreversible surgery (which I thankfully never got).

I tried to talk to my doctors about it but I couldn't' get an appointment for another six month and my latest round of testosterone blockers wouldn't wear off for another three. I was fast approaching the point two years in to hormone therapy where changes (including sterility) become totally permanent. So I decided to make my last irresponsible decision - go off hormones myself. I slowly lowered the dose of Oestrogen to last until the anti-androgen would stop blocking my testosterone production and when that ran out I stopped taking anything altogether. I am grateful I did this because a part of me had always wondered how manly I really was, how masculine I was naturally, was I producing testosterone like everybody else. I was in for a surprise. My testosterone production roared back into life and soon after that I went through possibly the most intense six months of my life. My facial and body hair began to grow back, my skin became oily and rough again, my shoulders and waist broadened out again but most surprisingly I became male again. I was angry, I was aggressive, I was horny all-the-time. All of those male traits I wasn't sure I really possessed became abundantly clear after two years of suppressing them. That was a big lesson for me - don't mess around with your body. Hormones or anything else. Once I was back on a level I decided not to go back to the Gender Clinic again, I wasn't sure I wanted to even afford them the time to lay into me for my irresponsible decision though deep down I think I was more concerned about their response to mysacrilege. After all they had allowed me to do this to myself, even pushed me to do it, without a minute of real counselling.

That's not to say the staff at the Gender Clinic are bad people, or that there aren't people who are genuinely trans. Research is showing there are a whole host of developmental abnormalities and circumstances that can lead to visibly or even less obviously intersex (both male and female on some biological level) individuals. But that doesn't mean we all are, and it doesn't mean the way to deal with uncertainty or difference is with medication and surgery. The trans game is a dangerous one and from my time in the system I fear that we are using a blanket approach that ultimately will do more harm than good to the vast majority of individuals we treat. Approximately fifty percent of trans people attempt suicide while around twenty percent tend to be successful - and those statistics don't change after hormone therapy or surgery. It's certainly enough to make me stop and think, and if I have learnt one thing from this, its that it's okay to be trans - but just because it's okay it doesn't mean you are.

Chapter 13

Dr Sid Lukkassen's views

This chapter is written by an academic and commentator, Dr Sid Lukkassen, who has written extensively on society, the fake news phenomonen, cultural marxism and political correctness.

I think the chapter on birth control hormones is fascinating. Whether true or not, or whether the results have been surpressed by big pharma and the women's movement, I don't know, perhaps others may conduct further studies – that is, if they can get a grant to do so. Because, as I have shown in this book, any studies that go against the 'facts' of Cultural Marxism is deprived of research funds – people lose their jobs and vicious campaigns are launched against them.

Sid's take:

War Is Peace – Freedom is slavery – man is woman Marxism is dead in the East but the Cultural Marxist hegemony of the West is nearly complete Hierarchies of victimization: androgyny in a declining West

An immense form of scepticism arose in the 1960s, which revolted against the church and families as leading forms of authority in those days. This was a societal form of scepticism; yet simultaneously a philosophical form appeared, which argued against objective knowledge and well-defined truths. This form of scepticism ranged from Jacques Derrida to Paul Feyerabend, from Woodstock to the Dutch Provo movement. On the ruins of that scepticism a mass-consumerism blossoms, as well as attempts to 'deconstruct' the basic facts of life – including biology. According to Theodore Dalrymple, the contemporary European lives on an inherited moral substance nurtured by the now-lost traditions of a previous generation. As this moral fabric is depleted, forms of *identity politics* arise to fill the void.

In 2015, the author Gabriele Kuby published *The Global Sexual Revolution: The Destruction of Freedom in the Name of Freedom*. She criticizes the idea that we can just change our sex – an ideology that permeates all of society down to the basic level of kindergarten. As the founding stones of this ideology, Kuby pinpoints communist doctrine, radical feminism and the leftist student revolutions of the sixties. Radical feminism in particular is aimed against women as mothers and life givers, simultaneously driving fathers away and devaluating masculinity. Through a 'long march through the institutions' these activists infiltrated public offices, global corporations, the academia and the justice system. In this chapter we will examine the long-term consequences of that infiltration.

First, we have to point out that Marxism developed differently in the East than it did in the West. In the West there was a functioning capitalist democracy: Marxists operated 'behind enemy lines' – their mission was to *criticize* from within the nation states operated by the bourgeois-capitalist system. The Eastern Marxists, by comparison, had a different mission: they served to *legitimize* the communist states that were part of the Soviet Union as being justified for being in accordance to Marx' teachings. This means that we have economic Marxism in the East and Cultural Marxism in the West. The failure of economic Marxism was laid bare by the fall of the Berlin Wall and the disintegration of the Soviet Union. Cultural Marxism on the other hand still thrives – surviving in the form of policies pursued by progressives, gender diversity activists and other social justice warriors.

Cultural Marxism and Fredric Jameson

Fredric Jameson, a Marxist literary critic, authored the book *Conversations on Cultural Marxism* in 2007, while Derk Jan Eppink mentioned Cultural Marxism in *The Wall Street Journal* in 2001. Branding this 'away with us' ideology as a 'conspiracy theory' is therefore based upon misinformation; quite the reverse – we observe that the ideology of the Frankfurt School positioned itself on fertile soil: the Christian way of putting oneself into perspective, the trauma stirred up by decolonization, the feelings of guilt towards the persecution of Jews, shame in Continental Europe about collaborating with the German invader; all this was put together by the Marxist struggle of the labour class and women's movement, during a period where mass consumption and increased mobility accelerated the cutting loose of traditional ties. As ordinary citizens, cultural Marxists look only marginal, yet the fertile soil for their agenda yielded an enormous long-term influence.

> "A *totalizing politics* is the only solution. I know there are people who object to this word, but one can point out that Jesse Jackson's Rainbow Coalition, for example, was very much a totalizing operation in which

Jackson never talked about women without talking about working-class women and about race; never talked about race without talking about class or gender; and that all of these things had to be done simultaneously."

Social engineering and utopianism

Jameson shows Cultural Marxism to be a permanent critique of capitalist and civic cultural values, which results in a political Rainbow Coalition of the previously mentioned 'marginals'. He promotes the deconstruction of "gender privileges" and therefore points at "Marxist feminism" and "utopian lesbian feminism." This "utopianism" is concerned with an all-encompassing form of *social engineering*.

The five-year old Jacob Lemai was initially born as Mia: her parents changed Mia's name to 'Jacob' when she displayed behavior atypical to girls. The LGBT movement portrays Jacob as a Messiah who may stimulate the acceptation of transgender children. But there are critical voices, like Dr. Paul McHugh, head psychiatrist at Johns Hopkins Academic Hospital in Baltimore. The results of his research suggest that 80% of transgender children could spontaneously lose their desire for gender change.

The quest for utopian social engineering reached its peak when GLAAD (the American LGBT lobby) launched a Twitter bot that searched the web for media referrals to 'he' as to specify Caitlyn Jenner, previously named Bruce Jenner. These referrals were corrected to 'she' – which also goes for past referrals in which Bruce was a father for six children. War is peace. Freedom is slavery. Man is woman.

Gender transgressions in music and entertainment

Whether it be Bruno Mars, who appeared with purple rollers in his video clip Uptown Funk, or Miley Cyrus, who approached her audience by wearing a prosthetic penis in The Riviera Theatre, the pattern remains unchanged. In fact, pop stars are mayflies who disappear as quickly as they acquired fame – if they wish to continue their existence they must transform.

This pattern explains why pop star Beyoncé dressed herself in leather lingerie when performing at the Superbowl in 2016; her gear included supportive signs for the racist and terroristic Black Panther group. Beyoncé acquired her fame through her ethnic status, her 'R&B' background that trained her to pump, grind and shake her booty like the flywheel of a steam engine. Every hint of femininity has been peeled away, leaving only a marionette show: a show played by Eros and Thanatos that keeps the masses entranced by their tubes. Exactly as the Roman gladiators of old, when the games in the arena served to discharge the social tensions of a declining world empire. From pop stars to sports heroes – we want our 'whores of Babylon' and they have to be mighty. The female desire to please – to be seen and admired – reaches the end of her transformation and at that point has cast off every trace of feminine vulnerability. What remains is a masculine Will-to-Power: unigender-fascism dressed in leather lingerie, including a prosthetic penis.

But before we attribute these examples to moral factors and the influence of Cultural Marxist coalitions, there is good reason to reflect upon the biological, chemical and hormonal factors involved.

Hormones and rat experiments

An intriguing article published by The American Thinker describes the influence of chemical elements upon the formation of sexual identities. The author refers to a CBS documentary about what happens to lab rats treated with sex hormones early on in their development.

He writes about an experiment with lab rats in the early 1960s:

> "These rats were given the synthetic hormones used in the then new birth control pills. The results showed that the grandchildren of these lab rats would have high rates of homosexual behaviors. The findings were suppressed – apparently, the powers that be wanted 'the pill' to pass muster. The first generation of kids born to mothers using the pill have already arrived. But we should expect in another generation a noticeable increase in homosexual behavior, so I was told in the mid'80s. By this reckoning, we should have seen a societal explosion of homosexualitystarting around 2000."

The author then proceeds to verify his observation with scientific references:

> "We have to ask ourselves, what happens to all those women using hormonal contraceptives when they stop their pills in anticipation of wanted pregnancy. Does the normal human cycle return immediately, or is there a rebound effect where, even if ovulation occurs, the ambient hormonal background in the womb is screwed up? This article addressed the question of whether gonadal steroid

exposure during prenatal development is one of the factors, in at least one of the pathways, that lead to variability in sexual orientation outcomes. Based on the compelling evidence that prenatal testosterone exposure influences children's sex-typical play behavior, on the well-established links between childhood play interests and adult sexual orientation, and on the evidence showing altered sexual orientation in women exposed to high levels of androgens prenatally, because of CAH, the answer appears to be 'yes'." (US National Institutes of Health)

"In addition, evidence has shown that women who are exposed to androgen early in life are more likely to identify as homosexual or bisexual." (Medscape)

"According to a newly released hypothesis, homosexuality might not lie in DNA itself. nstead, as an embryo develops, sex-related genes are turned on and off in response to fluctuating levels of hormones in the womb, produced by both mother and child. This benefits the unborn child, however if these epigenetic changes persist once the child is born, and has children of its own, some of these offspring may be homosexual." (SciTechDaily)

Thus, the lab rat experiments story has some scientific merit.

The destruction of the traditional family through economic means

Having charted both the cultural and the visceral factors that undercut the formation of traditional families in the current day and age, we turn towards the economic influences.

In the Netherlands, dismantling gender and class privileges is going berserk and has culminated into the marginalization of the position of men who are responsible for their families. Such is argued by Jos Teunissen, a Dutch Professor of Constitutional and Administrative Law: "If a working couple lives together and generates a total income of 40.000 euro – (two times 20.000) – then they must pay income taxes amounting to 1998 euro. A single working person without life partner who earns 40.000, loses 10.172 to public authorities."

According to Teunissen, this is a violation of human rights, as couples are not allowed to arrange for their economic household nor can they appropriately distribute chores among family members. Moreover, the more a man is engaged with managing domestic commitments, the higher the likelihood of divorce, according to social-psychologist Thomas Hansen. This conclusion is derived from research Hansen carried out in Norway. Dutch Minister Jet Bussemaker, who is in charge of the Education, Culture and Science portfolios in the current caretaking government, stated that men have to work less in the economy and more at home since women are experiencing less spare time.

Simultaneously, The Netherlands Institute for Social Research (SCP) finds it "striking to note that men with young children spend more time working than their peers without young children. Also, fathers with young children are more occupied with domestic commitments and care." Put simply, the working father is still the most productive member of our society. Women indeed massively opt for feminized office jobs that are centered around climbing the career ladder through office politics by gossiping and social games, instead of through output efficiency. Regrettably, our 'economy' is increasingly based on this type of job. The CEOs will not change this since they need such jobs to reward their corporate mistresses.

Effeminate fashion

Another striking example from the Netherlands is the adoption of gender neutral children clothing by the firm Hema. When analyzing the economic assault upon the classical definitions of femininity and masculinity, there is no force as lucrative as fashion:

> "Famous people often say that they want to do good for the world. And now I think: 'wow, I may have done something like that.' The twelve year old Julia wrote a letter to Hema two years ago, stating she found it silly that she could buy only panties with hearts on them. Today Hema revealed that they will scrap the sex descriptions upon the packages of the clothing."

Not only does this demonstrate Julia's apparent subjection to utopianism espoused by virtue signaling celebrities from a young age – it also perfectly connects with the same trends in clothing for adults.

As the photo above demonstrates, today's fashionistas are high-end hermaphrodites, whose luxurious lives are filled with cocktails that are consumed in private swimming pools (and in saunas visited by catamites). These *gender fluids* ask themselves how they can feminize Europe as quickly as possible. Even average labor-class men are expected to peel away their masculinity so that this continent can be gang-raped by nomadic groups from Africa and the Middle-East, where masculinity is regarded as a quality to strive for and experienced as a force to express.

This selective clique experiences a masochist temptation when forecasting the opening up of a femininely developed Europe to this extremely masculine influx. This elitist type of people is comparable to the group of 'Islam experts' nowadays: those who have visited gay bathhouses in Cairo during their student period – so I was told by a secular Turkish nationalist – and now speak highly about the moderateness of Islam. All together they now await the same destiny as Roman emperor Heliogabalus – who imagined himself to be an androgenic god, but was then brutally stabbed.

Victim-hierarchies

This onslaught against traditional families and the aesthetic of classical role models comes simultaneously with a *hierarchy of victimhood* – it is meant to supplant the moral vacuum bequeathed by the collapse of traditional role patterns, vestal virtues and homely values.

Jutta Chorus writes in *nrc* how there is good money to be made in the cult of victimhood: "Finally there is the category of sociologists who see themselves as representing a 'culture of long toes' (putting them out in the hope that somebody steps on them – moral outrage guaranteed). For these people every setback is a trauma, every misstep a depression. The pharmaceutical industry benefits: in the Netherlands, 2,5 million prescriptions for psycho-pharmaceutics are doled out."

We may also refer to the sociologist Frank Hermans, whose area of expertise is 'victimization'. He notes that the group of 'professional victims' keeps growing on a yearly basis. "They make themselves invulnerable in discussions, because they use their identity as a victim as a means of power." Hermans uses data from psychiatrists and other sources of professional help, and calls out an "excessive emancipation of emotion". Chorus concludes that the professional victims use their victim status everywhere: at the doctor's, the press, in court and in political theatres. In all these areas, suspicions of stimulant behaviour only fuel their feelings of indignation for being neglected and misunderstood.

As a symptom of the same exploitable oversensitivity to social inequalities, Free Pride Glasgow announced that 'drag queens' were no longer welcomed:

> "It was felt by the group within the Trans/Non Binary Caucus that some drag performance, particularly cis drag, hinges on the social view of gender and making it into a joke, however transgender individuals do not feel as though their gender identity is a joke,' the group said.
>
> 'This is particularly difficult for those who are not out and still present as the gender they were assigned at birth. While it was discussed whether we could have trans drag acts perform, it was agreed that as it would not be appropriate to ask any prospective drag acts whether or not they identified as trans'."

This statement put forward by the organization shows us the *Law of the Endangered Species*: transvestites constitute a minority and deserve our support, but *only* if the hurt feeling of transsexuals do not come into play – the latter is considered more endangered and more deserving of our special consideration: is therefore given a preferential treatment. It's even more fun when the lecherous displays of those parades collide with the religious purity of Muslim minorities, as we saw recently in London and previously in Sweden. There the clusterfuck was even bigger – and even more beautiful – as anti-racist activists came to the 'pride' to counter-protest.

All these dynamics prove what we can call a *hierarchy of victimization*, as confirmed by Joel Best: "During the 1960s, Americans became sensitized to victims and victimization; by the 1970s, there was a widespread ideology of victimization." Coinciding with the 'long march through the institutions' of Cultural Marxism, "this ideology gained acceptance in key institutions and created a victim industry – a set of social arrangements that now supports the identification of large numbers of victims." Playing into this "industry" there will be those who feel disadvantaged by society, and go to extremes to get their identities recognized.

In Canada, Kori Doty, who identifies himself as a person "without binary gender", challenged authorities to prevent the eight-month old Searyl from being assigned a gender. The child's file now includes a 'u', which means 'unassigned' or 'undetermined'. In Denmark, gender neutral kindergartens have been established that refer to children as being 'hen' instead of 'he' or 'she'. Meanwhile, London metro staff is no longer allowed to refer to travelers as "ladies and gentlemen." The Amsterdam municipality also stopped using the term 'ladies and gentlemen' – the same goes for the public transportation company NS, of which the Dutch government is the hundred percent shareholder. NS now uses the sexless phrase 'dear travelers' to address passengers.

Conclusion

Thus far there is nothing that keeps us together except an ideology of "agree to disagree", which until now seemed to hold the chaos at bay. But as the victimhood hierarchy and identity politics encroach, that ideology is failing: the permissive neutrality between the narratives is steady filled with dominant and mutually exclusive group identities. The victim industry, hierarchies of oppression and the long-term influence of Cultural Marxism, can only lead to Western civilization coalescing into atomized chunks that drift ever further apart.

Chapter 14

What women want and conclusion

What women really want – and it's similar to men Standing up for women – we've achieved equality, let us get on with our lives

The heresy of writing those words.

I, along with my many women friends and colleagues, are fed up being treated as special beings, being told they we are oppressed, that we need our own safe spaces, that we are being oppressed, not very educated and bullied by our men if we have the temerity to vote for a right wing party, that our daughters are more valuable than our sons, when we are encouraged to see men as predatory when all they do is wolf whistle at us, that their whistling is just one step from rape.

We are fed up with cultural Marxism being forced upon us by successive governments and unelected supra-national bodies like the European Commission, the United Nations, NGOs, Davos attendees, charities masquerading as lobby groups, the extremist trans people who attack everyone in a very violent way who doesn't agree with them. The idiots who tell us that girls playing with dolls or wearing pink clothing is wrong and that we are encouraging gender stereotyping or that our boys who play with guns are aggressive potential killers, and that we are encouraging male aggression.

We are fed up being told what to think, what to see, and how to act. Whether it's the Hollywood luvvies who, from their very privileged gilded cages live lives of extraordinary wealth and privileged, shielded from the harsh realities of life with the working classes, shit schools, urban deprivation, access to healthcare and living in ghettos who tell us that we should be doing. They lecture us to help more 'refugees' whilst refusing to house any themselves in their large mansions and multiple homes, gated and security protected. They say we should pay more taxes when most of them dodge taxes because of off-shore companies and dodgy investment schemes. They tell us to let your kids trans – they allow little boys called Shilo and Grubbucket to wear dresses and wonder why they go off the rails and into drugs or self harm? They're 'appalled' at Trump and Brexit because their cosy consensus run by their friends, the Clintons, the Bransons, the Clooneys has been shattered. They have invested time and money attending fundraisers, raising adopted kids imported from around the world, their PRs have been paid and made a fortune – and for what? The fairytale to be crushed by the hick, uneducated workers with votes. They shame us because we take an aeroplane for a couple of weekends and two holidays a year (if we are lucky), contributing to global warming while they flit about in private jets to lecture at climate change conferences or fly to multiple homes. They lecture us on carbon emissions in our gas guzzling cars whilst they inhabit the luxury world of the self-driven Ferrari or the chauffeur driven Maybach, whilst boasting on TV programmes that they drive a Toyota Prius. Frauds, all of them.

And politicians. We are fed up with politicians lecturing us on obesity, smoking, child care, sugar intake, drinking, parenting, green taxes, what to do in pregnancy. We want a small state, less taxes and for them to stop interfering in our lives.

We are better at spending our incomes on our families and lifestyles rather than big government interfering and mis-spending our hard earned cash on frivolous, expensive and quite frankly, wrong 'initiatives'. Trust us to spend our own money on what we see fit.

We want our judges to be able to deport foreign criminals rather than believing their human rights are worth more than those who have raped, murdered or robbed us. We do not want supranational bodies overriding our courts, like the European Court of Justice

We want our police to be able to their jobs properly without a culture of pansy political correctness. If they make a joke about bacon and Muslims, we don't want them to be sacked. Do not give them ridiculous 'targets' where they nick the easy target – the drivers – rather than wasting resources on this, they should be tackling real crime. Rather than chasing people online for politically incorrect remarks on the internet because some Snowflake is hurt, get those who are posting jihadi material online.

We want our judges, police and politicians to police our borders, protect our own people, not those who have entered our shores illegally. We want you to protect our kids from drugs as set out in my book, The Parents Guide to Drugs and how to start a war on drugs the politicians never started.

We want our schools to teach the skills that make us competitive and earn higher salaries in a globalised world. We want engineers, mathematicians, computer scientists, medics and scientists, not an army of people with 'ologies', media, wimmin or race studies degrees. These subjects divide people. There is a need for lower skilled workers like the service, beauty and hospitality industries. All worthy and rewarded roles, but we don't need the overeducated ologists to look down their noses at them. We don't need our teachers wasting time on gender and de-sexing and de-humanisation our children.

The sisterhood of the feminazis want us to be in charge of our own destinies but it is these same wimmin who form part of an industry who keep infantalising us and demeaning our men and boys. They cannot be trusted but they think the little women, those not educated in wimmin's studies, cannot be trusted to think for themselves. Even feminist, Camille Paglia, thinks that they should be defunded. In the US they were created to fill a void, the women were mostly taken from English faculties, have never taken into consideration biology as a fact and now are vessels of poison that have infected the UK too.

That's what we don't want.

We've achieved in education

In our schools girls achieve higher grades than boys, we outnumber the boys at university in 112 out of 180 subjects. Women outperform men at all universities.

Women outnumber men in medicine, law, history, philosophy, English and biology and 30,000 more women have signed up to university this year.

The feminazis are not happy, though. The bemoan the fact that female students make up the majority in nursing, psychology, social work, education and design. So what? We need nurses and, unfortunately because of socialism and social breakdown, more social workers. I don't care what sex they are, they just need to be able to nurse the sick and educate the kids.

Yet when we get to university/college the feminazis would have us believe that these hallowed halls have rapists and sexual abusers lurking around every corner. There are now mandatory sexual consent classes. They want trans people to share women only halls without thinking of the consequences for the real women with intact vaginas. Just wearing a Women's March vagina hat doesn't make you a woman, even if you have had your penis chopped off and fitted with a cavernous hole, without a clitoris or womb. They haunt our halls of learning.

As a woman and a mother, I am more concerned about the white working class boys that are under achieving at school and in the work place. Their female counterparts are, however, more likely to go to university.

I am concerned about the black kids because it is their culture that is holding them back, not because they can't learn at school. I don't want them specifically targeted and singled out, but their under achievement is cultural – gangs, drugs, errant fathers are the problems for black boys. And their mothers are concerned too, help them.

In the US, as well as the UK, free speech is being violently shut down. Our universities are inhabited by a majority of socialist lecturers who broker a zero tolerance discussion on any alternative view. Conservatives and Republicans, academics and philosophers are banned from speaking. Former 'radicals' are now banned because their form of feminism, politics, gender is offensive to the safe space Snowflakes.

University is no longer an arena for debate or thinking.

University is just used as an example. I do not oppose university, I just think there are equally honourable alternative pathways to learning skills.

Recommendation: A radical shake up of what and who we fund. Shut down the feminist and women's studies courses, limit the psychology courses and spend that cash on skills to improve our economy. I've never met a women's studies graduate who contributed to anything other than misery.

Hands off our bodies

Not a week goes by when we are not lectured about our bodies or companies shamed for not being PC in advertising campaigns using bodies.

As I have demonstrated in this book, ad campaigns are shamed and taken down from our screens and billboards.

We are constantly told that it is wrong to want to be slimmer, that's body shaming. I'm more fed up by those that think they can stuff all manner of crap down their throats and I have to pay the same as them to sit on an aeroplane, whilst their lard arses ooze out of the seats, their arms takeover my arm rest and they fat spread into my space.

We are told when pregnant that we shouldn't eat for two; we shouldn't drink alcohol; we should breast feed; we should be given carbon monoxide tests to see if we have been smoking. By whom? Interested and well-funded charities, whose only existence is there to lecture and shame us. And government departments staffed by the PC brigade who think that's what they should be doing to earn their money.

Men are told they cannot compliment us on our clothes, hair, shoes and make-up. Why not? If we are not dressing up and using these props to make us look and feel good, we are also using them to attract men.

There is a charity, Collective Shout – 'a grassroots campaigns movement against the objectification of women and the sexualisation of girls. http://www.collectiveshout.org/brands

There is never a grassroots campaign. Whatever their mission they are always very well funded, have great looking websites, fully of 'resources' and 'campaigns. One of their campaigns targets brands – think John Lewis, Clarks and others, in this book – and imagine you are the CEO and PR director for a corporate brand and these people target you. Your brand and image will be trashed, your stock will take a pounding and your staff will feel diminished. It doesn't matter that the company's advertising or sponsorship is what their focus groups and pollsters tell them is liked by the consumers – including women – they will trash you and make you change your approach. One of their recent campaigns is against that bastion of sexism and right wing thinking, the Wall Street Journal. They've been 'shamed' because they ran an ad for Stuart Weitzman shoes where women were hugging each other in high heels. I know, you're laughing, thinking oh, the hypocrisy of this. Yep, women hugging women and in high heels? Surely the sisterhood should be proud?

Enough! Give us the information we need to live healthy lives and look after our bodies and babies and we will do the rest. Trust us, we are the best educated generation yet.

Please do not de-sexualise us, we've fought for equality, not anonymity or androgeny

We are women, proud of our bodies (mostly), we are proud of being mothers (mostly) and attempts to air-brush our sexuality into androgeny is dangerous and wrong.

We want to be called 'mums', not 'parent', to use that in the plural term is good, but to airbrush women as mothers from your sanitised Marxist world is wrong. If gay men become parents, all well and good, they are not mothers, ie not female and not able to get pregnant and give birth. Those people that identify as men but keep their wombs for pregnancy are still women and 'mums'. Do not pretend otherwise.

As described in Chapter 4, the UK's Foreign and Commonwealth office have asked the UN to revise its guide to 'pregnant women' to 'pregnant persons'. I never thought I would say that a Conservative government was sounding more lunatic, left-wing and deluded and that even the UN is sounding sensible these days.

This is all being sneaked through. It is a sinister move without any thought of the implications and consequences for women, mothers, children, families, the men, fathers, brothers and biological facts.

Women do not want this. The fathers of the babies do not want this, the normal families of Great Britain do not want this. This ability to re-write biology at the stroke of a civil servant's pen has to be curtailed.

(Enormous thanks must go to the Sunday Times for exposing this) https://www.thetimes.co.uk/article/its-not-women-who-get-pregnant-its-people-w3mmzbgwh?shareToken=80953512d8f53d27d4932221689710b6

When science or evolution creates all humans as hermaphrodites, then that will be the time to de-sex us.

Do not ask us invasive questions at health consultations

The British NHS cannot be made to ask every person over the age of 16 years seeking a health consultation about their sexuality.

Imagine a little old lady, slightly deaf, a little bit of dementia kicking in when she is asked what her sexual preference is. 'What dear, sex? No, I gave that up years ago. Sorry, did you say what sex am I? Isn't it bloody obvious, I've got sagging boobs, I might have a bit of hair round my face but I'm not a bloke. Who are you insulting? Gender – what's that, love? My sexual preferences? None of your bloody business. I am here because I can't remember too well, my bladder isn't what it used to be and I can't walk as well as I did and you're asking my what my sexual preferences are, grow up lad and don't be so rude'.

The State does not need to infiltrate every person's privacy for a small minority. Records get lost, they get hacked, the information is given to other organisations. This is not the State's business.

First rule of government is to keep us safe

So why aren't you?

Up and down the UK vulnerable girls have been drugged, abused, raped and held as sex slaves by mainly Pakistani heritage men. Men of first or second generations who think that white girls are trash, are there to be abused for their merriment, business practices and sexual fun.

These girls lived in government care but when they complained to the authorities no one believed them because they were considered white trash and the sensitivities of perceived accusations of racism that might be levelled at these mainly white middle class apparatchiks were complicit in the abuse.

Local authority workers, the police, schools and social workers, all paid for by the UK taxpayer, to keep our vulnerable children safe decided by group think to adhere to decades of social change driven by socialist clap trap ideology to protect the perpetrators rather than the abused.

In one town, at least 1400 girls were used in a vast child abuse ring. They endured rape, threats, violence, child pregnancies, miscarriages and abortions. These poor girls were aged between 11-15 years.

A female socialist Muslim MP said that the victims should 'shut their mouths' for 'the good of diversity'. She is still in her job. Why?

The girls describe anal sex, rape, being drugged, gang raped, sexually transmitted diseases and worse. They said the police and social workers didn't believe them because they were white trash, slags and petty criminals. Some committed suicide.

Listen to Edmund Burke you leftist, conservative political cowards:

"The only thing necessary for the triumph of evil is for good men to do nothing." Edmund Burke.

Stop multiculturalism and integrate

When I stood for the UK Parliament in 2010 I was shocked that the majority of women over the age of 50 years of Bangladeshi and Pakistani origin could not speak English.

Knocking on doors in my constituency which had a 30% Muslim demographic, I could hardly find a woman over 50 who spoke English. There was another category of newly imported wives and husbands who also couldn't speak English.

I was taken to a tea party held in my honour by a 30-year-old university educated professional woman to meet a number of her community.

I asked her why her mother, aunts and older women did not speak English. She said, oh, but they did, when they came here 30 years ago. They had to speak English because they had no choice. When they shopped, took their children to school they had to learn otherwise they wouldn't get by. Now, as the years have gone by and there are more of us, we don't have to go outside of our community for shopping or schools, so they have forgotten how to speak English.

My friend also had two small children and a husband. Despite the fact that she was born in the UK, had been educated and went to university, graduated and had a good job in business, she had imported her husband, who didn't speak English and drove a taxi for a living. Why, I asked?

She looked uncomfortable and said there wasn't anyone suitable. What she meant and subsequently confirmed, were two things. One, a number of the men born here and of similar status had become too Westernised. The second reason was to import more people from their homeland.

This was confirmed further by knocking on more doors where the women were teachers, doctors, dentists, all professional women, with the inevitable taxi outside, for the imported husband.

How can you stop radicalisation if you cannot speak English? How can you understand what your child is looking at on the internet or what he is saying on the phone?

How do the feminazis square this?

In the same 2010 election campaign David Cameron honoured me with a visit. The usual protocol is for the leader of your party to visit for the photo op, the chat with the local and regional press and for you to show what good deeds you are doing in your constituency via a local charity or worthy cause. I was a past master at this having had the honour of organising such visits for Conservative candidates for the then leader of the opposition, Michael Howard.

Not Dave. He had visited a number of constituencies around the UK where the candidate had been side-lined. The visit wasn't 'political', no photo ops with the candidates, just of Dave, without suit and tie, sleeves rolled up, trying desperately not to look and sound too posh and too southern. And I was a woman. Dave liked women, but I suppose the right kind of woman – pro EU and pro immigration.

Dave was to march with a load of white middle class parents who wanted a school of their own, in their own area, which was slightly autonomous from the state.

Sounds good, eh? It does, until you understand why these parents wanted their own school. They wanted an apartheid in the white middle class area up on the hill, away from the mainly Muslim families in the valley below.

I told Dave that these parents were stirring up further education and cultural apartheid if he allowed this to go ahead. These schools also came with a separate pot of money. I told him that if you allowed these parents to have their own school then the Muslim parents will want their own state funded madrassas, was this acceptable? I told him that an Imam had already approached me to ask for separate status.

I was ignored by Dave.

In the same constituency a nice man called Mohammed became friendly with me and helped me on my campaign. I heard a lot about his wife and one afternoon I was taken to tea. I was curious why she never attended any social function. The excuse was 'she was looking after the kids'. A lovely lady, with little English, was looking after three boys in their late twenties.

I told Mohammed off. How can you honestly want to work with me on my campaign why you keep your wife at home, without English and using, three able bodied 'kids' as an excuse? I tried explaining about integration and what better way to heal the divide between our two communities was to socialise.

Janice, said Mohammed, you serve alcohol at your events. It is forbidden to us Muslims.

I told him to stop putting barriers in the way. He wanted to keep his little wife at home, without English, to serve his ideals. I was angry about the alcohol reference. Do you think we are going to make you drink, Mohammed? It is part of our cultural of socialisation and until we break down these barriers we are storing up more trouble and resentment for the future.

Campaigning one day my two lovely 18-year-old male interns were handing out my leaflets. One of them slid over to me, Janice, do I give a leaflet to the ladies in the burkas or should I just hand them to the men?

I was quite taken aback, almost speechless (not good for a politician!). I told him that this is our country and whilst we respect other cultures the day that any man, boy or woman cannot approach another in the street in the name of democracy is the day we have lost.

I told him to approach the women, look them in the eye (if you can, some of the burka'd women wore mesh over their eyes) and ask them if they would like to take of my leaflets. Never defer to the man, but offer him one too.

Again, I ask the sisterhood, where are they for these really oppressed women? As educated women we do not want to live in a parallel society.

I attended a hustings meeting, the only one where the hardline socialist sitting MP would debate me. He organised it in the centre of a Muslim area, inside one of their cultural community centres.

He got terribly excited when he accused me of wanting to ban the burka. At that time I didn't because I was more of a libertarian back then and believed in choice. This rattled him.

Now my views have quite altered. I believe the burka and headscarf are Islamic uniforms and used as a symbol of rejection of our western way of life and the countries they are choosing to live in. They subjugate the women. The men have control. Younger women are choosing to wear the burka too, as a two fingered political statement against us.

As women we are equal to the men, we have fought for our equalities long and hard. The Islamic way of life is alien to our culture, women's emancipation, education and a rejection of our values.

A few times when I offered my hand to shake I was rejected. I was told it was against their religion to touch another woman. The first couple of times it happened I was stunned and didn't know how to react. Then I did. I told them that I was standing for Parliament to uphold the values of my country, to protect our culture and part of that culture was to shake people's hands, whether you are male or female. I told them I was offended by their narrow, sexist and frankly undemocratic attitude. I think it lost me a few votes but at least I stood up for what I believe in and what the women before me had fought so hard for.

A young bus driver approached me. He had heard that the conservatives had a policy that new immigrants had to have a level of English before being admitted. Was this true? Yes, of course, don't you think this is a good idea I said? No, said the man, in broken English, my wife cannot speak English, she is living in Pakistan and why should she, she should be allowed in to be with me? That said it all. I told him his wife couldn't join him. I don't think I got his vote either.

If the Muslim men ... and women ... want to live in a separate community with Islamic dress under an apartheid system I suggest they go and live in Iran or Saudi Arabia.

We want our politicians to uphold our liberal democracy, rule of law and equality, not allow separate communities to live under the apartheid of multiculturalism. We want the feminazis to recognise this and support us.

Keep us safe by not importing more trouble

Keep us safe from the marauding migrants you have unleashed on us. You didn't ask for our permission to flood our European towns and cities with migrants that have no respect for women.

From Italy, Sweden, Norway, Germany, France, the UK and beyond. You have imported economic migrants, masquerading as refugees, who think white women are up for sexual assault and rape. You have had to produce leaflets telling them how to behave. You have turned a blind eye and even lied about what was really happening on our streets because you have no idea how to react to what you have unleashed. See my book, The Migrant Crime Wave, available at http://www.janiceatkinson.co.uk

And then they start to bomb us. Terrorism has also slipped across our borders with the migrants. It is estimated 50,000 potential terrorists have slipped in via the 'migrant crisis' you have created. You have no way of monitoring them all.

The first job of government is to keep us safe – nation state governments, the UN and the EU have failed us.

You have allowed festering Islamism to infect the minds of men who hate us.

The Ariana Grande bombing in Manchester was aimed at mainly young girls attending a concert with their friends and mothers. I have some sympathy of the school of thought that it was deliberately aimed at young girls which the sisterhood decried as the bomber being a misogynistic man. The reality is that in his sick mind he aimed it at scantily clad, amoral girls, enemies of the caliphate, bombing them would create the most outrage. Yes, he was misogynistic too, interpretation of his warped religion demands that of him.

By not having the personnel to hunt down these bastards because successive governments have cut back on policing, law enforcement, our courts, our forces and secret services, we are made unsafe. More so, our girls and mothers. We as women demand more.

In December 2018, the UK government signed the UN Migrant Compact. This allows for uncontrolled immigration from third world countries into the West. It also criminalises the terms 'illegal migrant', every illegal migrant is now a 'migrant'. This is an example of governments going against the national interest. A petition to discuss this in Parliament was signed by 130,000 people, 30,000 over the number necessary for debate. No debate took place. This single destructive act by a government that pretends that we will be taking back of our borders post Brexit, will condemn the UK to uncontrolled third world migration that will undermine our values, culture, laws and way of life. We did not vote for this.

Stop dehumanising, diversifying and making our police forces a laughing stock

Since Tony Blair was elected our police forces were forced to employ diversity officers and became subject to a tick box culture, lobotomised of common sense and were generally reduced to social workers rather than law enforcers.

Thankfully, most diversity officers have been made redundant but the culture of gender and race diversity is still omnipresent in the HR departments.

We don't care whether our officers are women, black, Asian or gay. We don't want you prancing around in the streets at music festivals pretending to get down with the kids whilst ignoring the drug dealing and taking which is endemic at these 'festivals'. Ignore the Black Lives Matter pretenders and the liberal left who accuse you of racism for tackling drugs and raiding drug dealers houses (when you do), you're there to keep us safe, not to see colour or race.

Male officers - we don't want you painting your nails with nail polish in an act of solidarity for Anti Slavery Day. Who wants slavery apart from the people traffickers and the alien cultures we have imported into our countries? Painting your nails doesn't release the Vietnamese women who are enslaved by traffickers to paint our nails. Instead, you should be raiding their salons and homes, arresting the traffickers and deporting the slaves.

Painting your nails and posting it on Twitter is time when you are not raiding the Albanian car washes that have sprung up all over the UK. Where guns, drugs, money-laundering and people trafficking is rife. Stop painting, start arresting, charging and deporting.

Government, our police officers double up as social workers for the mentally ill, drug and alcohol dependant on our streets because your failed policies haven't kept up with the mental health and dependency units needed for this population. You haven't trained the social workers needed to cope with them, instead you rely on our crime prevention system for cleaning up. Instead, our police should be spending more time on prevention and catching criminals rather than cleaning up your failed social mess.

Please tell successive faux conservative home secretaries that you are not going to police hate crime, misandry and misogyny. The majority of women who haven't been brainwashed in gender studies and university safe spaces can argue our case and we don't mind wolf whistles. We are not going to commit a regressive hate crime by reporting some man who slapped our bottoms thirty years ago to ruin his life just to give us headlines. He may be dead, we are not going to ruin his family's memory of him.

We want you to police our streets.

We object to being frisked like a jihadi wife

Governments, you can't keep us safe by directing apparatchiks at security points to frisk all white women.

How many of us have felt the indignity of being treated like a jihadi wife at security points when travelling through an airport, or other point of exit?

I travel a lot for business, at least once a week I go through an airport via Eurostar rail services from England to the EU.

Each week at Eurostar I am checked for explosives. My underwired bras are thoroughly fingered for explosives, my shoes – with glass/glitter/shiny metal heels – are scanned for bombs, my waistbands and pants are snapped and I am routinely asked "is that your bra?" when their handheld scanner pings – all in sight of other male travellers and Eurostar staff and customs. Every week.

When I go through airport security I have the indignity of having to take off my shoes – occasionally I will have a hole in my sock or stocking which embarrasses me slightly, which get dirty walking on the floors and through the scanners. My bags are checked for drugs/explosives and sometimes my waistbands are frisked when they lift up my top to reveal my bare stomach, the tops of my pants and stockings.

Occasionally, I fly on a low cost airline or take my luggage on-board. Why is my hormone replacement therapy, whose lovely gel is dispensed via a large plastic pump action tube (to deliver happy hormones, sigh) questioned and threatened with confiscation by a spotty youth who has no idea what HRT is. 'Have you got a doctor's letter? No? Oh, I will have to confiscate that'. Whoa, get your dirty little hands of my hormones. The silly little see-through plastic bags which holds nothing more than a mini deodorant and toothpaste tube, cannot accommodate my hormones. Again, the majority of us, and particularly middle aged women are subject to demeaning and embarrassing questions and searches because governments do not have the courage to stand up and call out the scum who are the real threat.

Government – you are not protecting the public. You are wasting resources by trying to show you are not profiling and offending minority groups who may identify or have sympathy with ISIS. You are offending the majority. Stop it.

Let's stop silly # naming/shaming/guilt

#Metoo is currently trending where women are admitting to some form of unwanted attention or even rape. Some men are being asked to declare that they are not rapists. The majority of men are not rapists, sexual predators nor monsters we should be frightened of. Men: do not play along. It is demeaning and nasty.

The nasty liberal swamp dwelling elite are having a tough time after the Weinstein affair. Their answer? Hashtags. What do our sons think? They are being shamed to think that their fathers, brothers and heroes are all demented sex fiends. That their mothers, sisters and all women are afraid and victims of men.

This hysteria is becoming like the Salem Witch trials, feeding on a social media frenzy. No man is now safe. This is not what we want for our husbands, friends and sons. Corporates are now hanging our men out to dry for a public execution of those 'accused' and remember, all they need to do is 'accuse', those men are being very publicly drummed out of their jobs.

Sexual assault does not mean being groped in a taxi by your date; nor do sexual overtures from a drunken colleague who fancies his (or her, remember equality girls?) chances in a bar and neither should we be told we cannot compliment a colleague.

Women accept that if we can have it all, then those of us who think we are the same as men – both in sex, work and play, then we have to play by equal rules.

What is really sad is that we have achieved so much but now the tables have turned on our men and sons. It is up to the women on the Right to reverse these despicable acts of turning on our opposite sex.

Has the sexual revolution made us happier? It's certainly zapped our fertility

Women wanted to have control over their bodies, the freedom to choose when to have sex for pleasure and when to have sex for babies, to have the choice of one or the other has been one of the greatest emancipations of women in the West.

But we have paid a price. Fewer babies are being born in the West, less among women with degrees and a falling birth rate leads our political masters to decide that what we need is immigrants to fill that void, rather than tackling the root causes of decline. See my comments on the UN Migration Compact. Both the UN and EU are replacing our populations. Firstly, by telling us not to have more children to save the planet, then deciding that we need migrants to replace the babies we are not having.

We are told we can have it all and we do, including ageing ovaries and menopause – which doesn't keep up with the botox and fillers to smooth out our creases that age (and stress) brings.

We are leaving it later to have babies and that has consequences. IF we can find a suitable male mate and after we have paid off our student debts, and after we have had it all climbing the corporate ladder, we will have a baby. But it's not so simple because our hormone and fertility levels start to decline at aged 30, by 35 it jumps off a cliff and by 40 only 20% will be able to do so.

Women see celebs having babies in their 40s and tales of some in their 50s, thinking they can do it too. What the celebs and the expensive fertility clinics do not tell you is that around 65% of IVF fails. There are even fertility shows. Where once we might attend a large event venue to choose our next holiday destination, there are now shows dedicated to fertility. It goes hand in hand with our ageing mothers.

Education at school needs to change. Instead of PHSE classes dedicated to contraception, abortion and diversity, the stark facts of the lifespan of an ovary should be included. Contraception does have its place but so does fertility. If we do not we are letting down our girls and the next generation of mothers.

> *"To have a right to do a thing is not at all the same as to be right in doing it."*
> GK Chesterton (from *A Short History of England*)

The same as candles, teddies and # after terrorist atrocities. #ditchthehashtag

Hillary champion of women's rights?

The biggest sex scandal was President Clinton. With the alleged affairs, rapes, abortions, the naming and shaming of his victims (victims when he turned against them or when Hills found out). This happened in the Democrats! If the Democrats are such a women supporting party, why did they allow the biggest hypocrite for the sisterhood to stand as their presidential candidate? Why did the MSM give him airtime and her the red carpet? That's not what women want. Ask any abused wife. Yet the first lady of hypocrites was allowed to stand. Couldn't they find anyone better qualified, who got elected, the hard way, on her own merits?

We don't want to be lectured by the feminazi elite

No more gender elite books should be bought to 'self help' ourselves in the workplace or our relationships.

These books are written by an industry educated in wimmins studies that have spawned a middle class elite that is out to get our men and sons. These are the women that call meetings to discuss their 'issues'. The meeting rooms are booked by other women down the food chain, their catering is provided by other women even lower down the food chain, the offices are cleaned by other women even further down the food chain, to discuss 'issues' in their narrow little lives, that have no bearing on the women who serve them. They don't even think twice about their chain below.

Too much attention has been given to a minority that has targeted women working in the creative arts industries who have been given an enormous platform to shame other (formerly sensible) corporates to re-write their in-house personnel manuals, involve corporate responsibility departments and gone into PR overdrive with equality statements.

Human Resources departments should ignore the terms: mansplaning, micro-aggressing, manspreading and manteruption .

They should also ignore the cries from the wimmin for our menopauses to be taken into account. If the feminazis have truly won equality then we are they now playing up our hormones? Didn't we fight against men who claimed our tantrums, crying and inability to perform functions were down to hormones? We can't have it both ways.

We do not want our state broadcaster to indulge in cultural revolution group think

Those of you in the US are so lucky not to have a state broadcaster, paid for by the taxpayer. You might look at our BBC and think good thoughts, how lucky the Brits are to have it. Who wouldn't love our nature programmes, most children's TV, music, drama and some reality? When they do nature and drama it is truly magnificent (although Netflix and Amazon are nipping at their heels). But what women object to is the cultural revolution they are spearheading.

The BBC is run by a highly educated political elite, whose director general admitted that the BBC is inherently biased against conservatism. It is run by men who inhabit the north London dinner party circuit who think that Marxism is the new zeitgeist. The woman who are promoted to the top are gender quotas and woe betide you if you step out of line on their global warming theory, socialism, diversity, positive discrimination and luvvy virtue signalling. Woe betide you if you are a women of the right, you're labelled as racist or slightly bonkers. Brexit coverage is dangerously anti with little balance from the opposing view. Analysis has shown that during the Brexit campaign the BBC aired two thirds more anti Brexit voices than pro Brexit. There are more mockumentaries and documentaries on vilifying the right and if you're a right wing comedian, no chance.

The BBC is the dominant culture force and gatekeeper to modern life. Its online platform has put local newspapers out of print, its global audience is growing and isn't being used as a global platform for Great Britain.

As we leave the shackles of the EU, the BBC should be loud and clear about its patriotism, our flag, our open culture for business and life, our talent and industry, to shout and loud that we are open for business and act as a proud publicly financed force for good. Should be used to promote Global Britain.

Its constant whinging about why Brexit will fail, its open dislike for Trump whose highly paid and highly educated journalists sneer as his money and his gaucheness, is a platform for a lesson on how not to deliver news and how Britain can't be great (so last century darling, all that trading, money and spreading our language and culture, urgh) is letting us down.

Instead, we have to endure its dedication to delivering multiculturalism, diversity, equality and gender quotas. It doesn't hide its dislike of conservatism, it openly pushes drug legalisation and pushes injustice towards our men and sons.

When a recent tragic fire at a London tower block killed at least 80 people and uncovered the illegal sub-letting in the social housing tower, mainly to illegal immigrants, the outrage wasn't at the illegal sub-letting, or the lack of charges brought against the immigrant whose fridge was the cause of the fire with manslaughter. No, it was for the illegal immigrants who had all disappeared or were lying about their immigration status. The voices at the BBC were pushing the voices of those who were calling for an amnesty, housing and benefits for those illegal immigrants. Those calling for the upholding of the law were nasty, racist scum.

The BBC promoted the increase in hate crime brought about by the Brexit vote. The UK's unelected EU Commissioner, Julian King, quoted statistics and examples, aided by the liberal left of the Parliament's MEPs and the UK's right and left anti Brexit politicians. I was furious. I intervened and called him and them out by producing statistics and facts that showed them to be so dangerously wrong. Did I get airtime on the BBC? No, they are still pushing this public disinformation.

White people are bigoted racists, particularly those who voted for Trump and Brexit. We are responsible for hate crime and hate thought, we are responsible for attacks on nasty foreigners, even Hillary Clinton is joining in, her hate figure is MEP Nigel Farage and friend of Donald Trump. Feted and fawned over by the BBC she was given an inordinate amount of time on the BBC.

And then the biggest penis of them all, Bill Clinton arrived in the same week, to discuss Northern Ireland's peace agreement. Not content with pushing the EU's view about Brexit and that if a solution wasn't found for Northern Ireland's Brexit process, the Good Friday agreement would break down. Instead of pointing out that the IRA's guns would once again wreak havoc because it was being provoked by the

EU and encouraged by Western politicians that this was the likely outcome (ie if Northern Ireland didn't split from the UK and become a United Ireland), the BBC promoted this view. They did not point out that it was the will of the people that brought peace. Clinton was given prime time TV.

They push Populism, disguised as Nazism as sweeping Europe. When I went on TV to discuss the recent French presidential election. It was all they could do to stop prodding and poking me to see if I was real, do fascists bleed, she's a *friend of Le Pen!*

There is some justice. The BBC's 'flagship' programme on BBC Radio 4, 'Today', has lost over 1m viewers in the last year. I wonder why?

This agenda, including the subversion of our children's minds – transgenderism is normal – is letting us down. It is letting Britain down.

What about funding a Conservative women's forum or think tank?

A few years ago a Conservative – who is now in the House of Lords (via Cameron) and I launched WomenOn … a think tank dedicated to this book's agenda. We were so popular because we were saying the things that women wanted to hear. Across the BBC we were given airtime against the liberal gender benders and fawned over in the right wing press. I was nominated as woman of the year by the columnist Quentin Letts because we took on the perceived wisdom of the liberal left.

Yet we failed. There were two reasons, one is fact and one is my own thought.

We failed because we couldn't secure funding. Most funding of political forums/action groups/think tanks/campaigns is funded by old, rich white men. They just didn't get WomenOn. They didn't get our culture wars. They were obsessed by taxation and getting a Conservative government in place. Whilst this was our imperative too, they didn't see the diversity/equality agenda creeping up on them.

My other thought was that my partner was on the slightly left of the Conservative party and had been promised a seat in the House of Lords (I wasn't quite the type, too right wing). Dave interviewed her as a Downing Street women's advisor (really) and dangled a title in front of her. She ditched WomenOn.

The realisation that we need to tackle the culture wars has finally been recognised. We have a long way to go.

Our boobs have achieved. To bare or not to bare our breasts? Depends on who you are, of course

There are good boobs and bad boobs. Good boobs are displayed by nice middle class gels in nice upmarket magazines, even better if you are Hollywood royalty.

Bad boobs is objectification and exploitation of the under-educated in tabloids and low market magazines.

I defended the right of the UK's red top working class, best selling, cheap tabloid newspaper, The Sun, to keep it's famous Page 3 bare breasted girls. Mostly read by men, it is harmless and its women readers really didn't care. However, the wimmin campaigned and won to have the breasts removed from the paper. The downside was a lot of blond, working class, busty girls lost their jobs. (The wimmin also now hate the tabloid because it is right wing, encouraged Brexit and is owned by villain Rupert Murdoch).

The wimmin complained that Page 3 was sexual exploitation.

Now enter stage left another scenario.

When right-on actress (or is it actor?), and particularly the special ones, who are also UN Ambassadors of Goodwill – Ms Emma Watson, bare their breasts, they are truly shocked when their breasts are brought into play.

This little madam, when invited to preach in the hallowed chamber of horrors, the European Parliament, declined the invitation because she didn't have the time to turn up to fulfil her Ambo role to preach to the mostly converted in the European Parliament (Jean Claude Juncker, the EU Commission's unelected idiot, has nothing on Voldermort), but she had time to pose semi-topless for Vanity Fair and on the front cover of Vogue.

Ms Watson, was 'quite stunned' when she was criticised for getting her tits out, she wittered on … 'Feminism is about giving women choice', she said. 'It's about freedom, it's about liberation, it's about equality. I really don't know what my tits have to do with it.'

This outburst really sums up the warped feminazi's view of what equality really is. Of course the wimmin were quick to defend young Ambassador Watson's boobs saying that middle class right on PC women are ok for publicly baring their boobs. So is it ok for Watson to bare her boobs if it takes place with the backdrop of society magazines, dressed in designer gear?

No, it's double standards. Again, the middle class, educated feminazis defend their own but not the choice of the glamour models, women who are also making a buck because they're attractive.
Ms Watson has quite a lot to learn about how she is being manipulated by the feminazis, the UN and Hollywood. She cannot lecture the rest of us about politics and feminism if she doesn't understand choice – across the class divide.

If we have faith, protect us, if we are secular, protect us

Faith is important to people, from whichever religion. But when our beliefs are challenged in a court of law we should all be outraged, particularly if it is protecting a small minority over the majority.

In this book I have stood up for our Western Christian heritage, despite having no faith myself. But I will absolutely defend my cultural Christian heritage and for people of faith to live their lives according to their scriptures, but ours has supremity. And that goes for Muslims, Jews, Hindus and everyone else. To criminalise people because of their faith when pandering to sexual minorities has no place in our society.

And if you live in our Western countries and you are of another religion you must abide by our laws and customs. We will accommodate you as best we can but you have chosen to live in our countries so respect our cultures because ours has supremacy over yours.

We've achieved in salaries

Mind the gender pay gap – are we really paid less than men?

We are constantly being bombarded with the information that women are paid less and are valued less than men. But this is another campaign to exploit us, not help us.

As Jane Austen said: 'it is a truth universally acknowledged that men get paid more than women'. But do they get paid more than women for doing the same job? That's harder to answer.

In the UK we have had 'equality' enshrined in law since 1975 and in the States they have had various laws passed since 1964. Then why are we having the same arguments? In the UK the so-called gender pay cap is now down to less than 10%. Does it matter?

In the UK the socialists had bouts of power where all 'inequalities' should have been obliterated. So why do we have dinner ladies (sorry, catering people) dishing out school dinners and suing their employers for discrimination because they do not earn the same as, for example, the men emptying the bins? Same level of skills demands the same level of pay. And in mainly socialist run local authorities.

The inconvenient truth for all Western societies is that women tend to earn less than men because of part-time work (choice), type of occupation (choice) and having and caring for children (choice and some basic biological facts).

Another fact: women entering into the workplace tend to earn more than their male counterparts. Women between the ages of 22-29 years in the UK, will typically earn £1,111 more per annum than her male counterparts.

However, those sour faced pussies at the campaigners for wimmin, the Fawcett Society (not one man on their governing board) said: "Women have been suffering from the economic downturn more than men because they had even less job security … They were more at risk and thus worse hit when the recession struck."

She suggested more needed to be done to persuade young women to take up apprentices in better-paying industries. "Women are steered into roles like caring, beauticians and so on. These are poorly paid roles. We need to do more to steer women into non-traditional roles, or at least make it clear to them what these pay."

I guess she hasn't read the facts on girls' education attainment and university statistics, as detailed above. Of course she hasn't. If she had she would be out of a job.

Can you see the other agenda here? They sneer at jobs in beauty and caring. Beauty is a huge growth industry and the girls have to train for three full years, hardly an unskilled job. We are in desperate need of carers for our elderly and sick. What isn't noble about these. It's just another excuse to import cheap third world labour.

Women have made enormous strides over the past decades that our mothers could only dream of. We have been through universities, we are earning more than the men, we are taking our places in the boardroom because of this shift in education and working patterns. We do not need belittling gender quotas.

Women can have it all, can't we? But what do we do about babies?

Until the feminazi scientists can find a way for men to have babies – and I don't mean the trans types who self identify as a man but have kept their ovaries – women will continue to have babies. A bit of an inconvenient truth for the wimmin.

Until then they will complain and campaign and give us dodgy statistics on the motherhood pay gap.

They present the pay differences as some misogynistic plot from the men in the boardrooms against working mothers. Instead, it comes down to career patterns, the choice to work part-time. It's nothing to do with being a woman, or being a mother, or the primary carer, it comes down to changing work patterns, being out of the labour market and choosing not to work. There has to be trade-offs in a family. Who works, who looks after the kids, whose earnings are put on hold during the child's early years. It's family decision.

Women (correction, families) have never had it so good. In my mother's day there were no nurseries, today's childcare industry is booming, if expensive.

We do make it hard on ourselves. Families choose to be competitive helicopter parents, shuttling the kids between lessons in violin, piano, ballet, sports and parties. If you don't join in, making your own cakes for a cake sale (disastrous in my house), or making little Johnny's batman outfit, rather than buying one from the shop. No lie-ins on a Saturday morning because there's football or your plain dumpy little girl has to get her tutu on. Then there's the birthday party in the afternoon, more upscale, expensive presents and the drive to and from the party. Forget Sundays, there's homework to be done or more paid-for activities. Want a snooze in front of the TV after lunch? No, more children's parties or its organised play dates in your house where you are expected to participate.

It's hard work without the gender pay gap brigade carping on about how you've been shafted in your pay packets. The real enemy is the helicopter parent world.

Leave us alone to make our own choices, to work or not to work. Don't make us feel that we are letting down the sisterhood by being stay-at-home-mums.

Yes, there should be more flexibility in the workplace but don't undermine bosses if they offer a lesser job to a returning parent (of either sex) after time out to look after the family. Do not expect those employers to keep your job open, they're running a business not a lifestyle choice for you.

We've achieved in politics

I took a group of constituents to the European Parliament recently. A terribly nice and well educated young man (degree, languages, well paid), was despatched to speak to my group about the workings of the Parliament, including prepared charts and graphs on statistics.

Two things about this presentation. One, he was too educated for the job and two, that as I walked in to take up my space before speaking to my audience, he started speaking about the gender gap and how only 37% of MEPs are women, that must change, he stated. He follows a script.

I have great regard for the employed people of the Parliament, it's the institution I despise. I challenged this young man to ask why he thought 37% of women was not enough? He didn't answer. In spite of the fact that the EU has imposed gender quotas in most countries (except the UK, whose parties impose their own, save for one or two), they refuse to accept that women may not want to go into politics. Instead, the gender quota has allowed PC, wimmin's studies graduates and career politicians to infect our law making.

Strong women go into politics, it's no place for snowflakes. We have to be held accountable and in public – there are not many jobs where that is required. We have to be adept at debates and under fire from journalists who, like the US, try to trip us up, play politics like a game show, rather than have a grown-up discussion. It's like being a Gladiator thrown to the lions sometimes – and I am no wilting wallflower.

It's an equal playing field, so I would say to women who want to go into politics – do a proper job first, whatever you choose, get experience of life, paying taxes, whether you're a nurse of a captain of industry. Be under no illusion, it's hard, it's long hours, your enemies really hate you, the press are worse, be prepared to be in the spotlight, your friends and family too, there is nowhere to hide. Be prepared to be criticised for your clothes, hair, make-up and shoes – the assault is worse online – but you will also get compliments, take them and be proud. There is no sisterhood, it's a cut throat world, the sisters will climb over you with their kitten heels or trainers, to get to the top. Some men will make your life difficult, some will leer at you, that's life, human nature that no amount of feminazi bullying will stamp out.

When one former MP and icon, Ann Widdicombe, discussed feminism she identified with the 1970s feminism, as most of us do, because it gave us opportunities, we'll show the men we are just as good as you, if not better. Her take on 1990s feminism where women entering parliament for the first time, socialist women, were saying, 'it's so awful how the men speak to me'. Ann pointed out, 'yes, isn't awful how they speak to each other too?'

In the 2017 election the UK elected more women. The socialists have 45% and the Conservatives 21%. The feminazis cry foul, but is it all it seems?

The socialists have a policy of gender quotas, the Conservatives do not, although under Cameron there was a bit of gerrymandering going on to get the 'right kind of women'. Although the useless and irrelevant liberal party had all its women wiped out in 2015. Which goes to prove women don't vote along gender lines, they vote for the party and/or candidate. Despite the gender quota system, the socialists have failed to elect a female leader or indeed a prime minister. The Conservatives have had two, without a gender quota in sight.

How are they doing in the States? The same as the Conservatives, at 21%.

Stop campaigning for women to vote for other women. We don't vote with our vaginas, we vote with our heads.

I am so thankful every day that we didn't get President Hillary Clinton. Thank you.

Identify as trans? ... you're not a woman, don't ask for special treatment

There's something to be said for the binary majority. The vast majority – more than 99% - are happy in the normal gender spectrum – male, female, gay – of daily life. Being part of the gender binary majority simplifies the daily life of everyone. Clothes shopping, sports teams, passports, census collection, schools and even the way a bartender asks for your order. Why add the complication/crime of 'misgendering'?

What should we do ladies?

We need to fight back and tell them that we are strong, intelligent, capable and powerful and in charge of our own destiny. Identity politics is a very narrow, demeaning and destructive phenomena.

Stop the gender wars against ourselves, our men and our boys.

Tell our girls that useless subjects as universities and colleges such as gender and race studies as degrees are not worth the paper they are written on, literally. You will earn less, will just argue amongst yourselves, will be poorer intellectually, financially and socially, because it really doesn't matter. We are equal, let's lead our lives according to what we want.

Please bear in mind that we need to have babies to keep the human race going.

Women are defined by our actions, what we say and do, our relationships in our home, our businesses and our communities. If the feminazi wimmin actually asked what real women want, rather than the narrow orbit in which they operate, they might learn something. One thing which would definitely happen is that the feminazis would no longer have a platform.

Conclusion

The biggest losers? The women themselves

It seems to be the biggest losers in all this are women themselves. Often angry and sometimes violent these extremists who are punching and screaming their support for the women trapped inside male bodies, being oppressed by their genetics are actually harming women in general. It's not just the privacy of every woman, school girl, mother and grandmother in the country that is being trampled over; it is their basic human rights. The rights that were fought for and won by the suffragettes.

Modern society is so keen to balance the sexual books with positive discrimination … women only short lists, more women on boards of FTSE 500 /Wall Street companies, equal pay, breaking glass ceilings etc, etc. Now though it's seen as the men who can have it all. Well when I say men, I actually mean a man, someone who was born a man, physically looks like a man, dresses like a man and genetically is a man; but all he has to do is say 'I'm not sure about my sexuality, my inner woman is being oppressed' and hey presto he is now a 'new woman'.

The transwomen go to extraordinary lengths to look like sexy women. Facial surgery, fillers, botox, hair extensions, surgery to enhance 'breasts', bottom fillers, hormone pills, all done to what they see as enhancing their femininity, TV airtime and their bank balances. Yet, that's not how the majority of women see themselves or indeed want to be. No matter how much they fill, plump, primp and try, they are not real women. It's an insult to real women.

With this new found world of bathroom opportunities a 'new woman' can now fill that slot for positive discrimination. Whole boardrooms can change gender in a blink of an eye, and get to retire earlier too. Leading sportsmen across the country can become 'new sportswomen' and in many cases push the traditional ladies off the podium, plus get to share the same showers whether the original clientele like it or not. It will be interesting how the International Olympic Committee handle the whole transgender arena before the next Olympics. What will the conservative Muslim nations have to say about competing and touching angle of sport?

If we allow the extremists to win the battle, real women and men lose out.

We are at a tipping point in the West.

Populism is on the rise. Why? Because ordinary people are sick and tired of the old way of the cosy consensus politics. Right or Left, it's all the same, you might pay a little more tax under one, but the opposition when they get in power will still tax you more, it will just be dressed up differently with a separate label. The people recognise this.

If we do not have more family friendly policies to protect and support the family and give into the globalists who want to impose cheap, uneducated migrants upon us, then we can say goodbye to our Western values, culture and way of life.

How do you think these new imports will react to transgender policies? They hate homosexuals; women working and women in politics. What do you think they will make of trans people?

And our own children and young people? The result of this Frankenstein experiment by a minority for the majority will be a huge backlash. These kids will sue the authorities and the parents for messing with their minds and bodies.

What about our sons and daughters? They are equal. But in today's feminazi world, our boys are being demeaned and told that girls should be at the head of the promotion table and for 'equality's sake' they should be given more opportunities than our sons. I don't want a world that demeans fifty per cent of the population. Girls have every equal opportunity, if they choose to be a hairdresser rather than an engineer, that's their choice, so be it.

Western politicians need to back off micro managing our lives. They need to stop pushing agendas that harm and offend the majority.

The police need to fight for their numbers and to be left alone to police, not to give into becoming superannuated social workers and social society monitors and loggers of hurty tweets.

The Churches need to look after their brethren and to preach their doctrine, and get out of politics. Is it any wonder the Church of England's pews are empty and the Afro-Caribbean and the happy-clappy churches are thriving?

Our media is demonising working class people as 'Far right'. A re-calibration of narrative and factual reporting is required. A more balanced and less shrill approach to Brexit is also needed. Stop demonising Leavers as xenophobic, racist, uneducated, little Englanders. Less airtime should be given to the anti-democratic People's Vote crowd. They are not grassroots campaigners, they are well funded middle class people with a lot of money. They are a minority. Why do the media think they are being demonised and mis-trusted? The controlling of so-called Fake News and the bending of reality is dangerous.

Social media giants cannot be regulators of thoughts and feelings. They cannot oppose and shut down free speech, only direct threats of death or terrorism should be banned.

Our NHS needs to respond to our clinical needs, not the needs of a tiny minority who want a sex change. Infertile women and the elderly should be given priority funding over social wants.

No wonder people have had enough.

The EU Parliament has elections in 2019. The Federalists have had a terrible election cycle in the past eighteen months, which is set to continue into their elections in May 2019. The Socialists are expecting 50% loss of seats, along with a total wipe out of liberals, including Guy Verhofstadt and Merkel's group expect 25% losses. Learn from your mistakes. If you don't listen to the people they will not listen to you.

Populism is in its early stages, but it's storming Europe and the US. Voters were angry, so they just changed their political leaders, all under the radar of the establishment. Expect more. Delicious.